In their new book, Chrys and Shellie will remind you about what you're good at, inspire you to do what you're passionate about, and figure out what will outlast you. When you turn the last page, you'll want to go do these things for your kids. This book is one for the ages.

MARIA GOFF, wife, mom, grandma, and author of *Love Lives Here*

Being a grandparent ROCKS. Watching my friends Chrys and Shellie share about grandparenting rocks as well. I love the way they honestly and transparently share about their families. And in whatever season these two find themselves, they share that journey with the rest of us. Honored to call them friends. Now . . . LET'S ROCK! Serve well! Love big! It ALL matters!

SANDI PATTY PESLIS

Food, family, fun, and faith combine beautifully in this offering from the hearts and minds of two women who know the business of grandma love inside and out.

LISA WINGATE, #1 *New York Times* bestselling author of *Before We Were Yours* and *The Book of Lost Friends*

I adore this book! Not only did I feel encouraged by the gentle Solomon-esque wisdom for nurturing thriving relationships with my own five grands offered by girlfriend-authors Chrys and Shelli ⋯⋯⋯ by their hilarious and often poig⋯ that are drawn from the⋯

It Grand motivates us sweetly ripened gals (and guys!) to remain vital *people* with our own interests as we age. Who wants to rattle around like shucked corn husks after harvest? Not me! Not you! This awesome little book will help us bound out of our rocking chairs and seize priceless opportunities to teach our progeny by example . . . and when necessary, to use words! *Rocking It Grand* gets my highest commendation.

> **DEBORA M. COTY,** multiple award-winning author of over 40 inspirational books, including the bestselling Too Blessed to Be Stressed series, with over 1.3 million books in multiple languages worldwide

Chrys and Shellie have reminded me that we grandparents are "game-changers"! Not only that, but we can "raise the ceiling" for our grandkids! Matter of fact, our ceiling becomes their floor to walk on and live out our legacy. Our works/legacy will outlive us (Revelation 14:13)! Nice to know that we can "set the stage" for those coming after us! This is FUN FAITH!

> **DENNIS SWANBERG,** America's minister of encouragement

Rocking It Grand feels like I'm sitting on the porch listening in as two wise women share wisdom, faith, funny stories, and recipes. I walked away with a buffet of inspiration and instruction to call on as I walk out my Grand journey—oh, and an amazing host of cookie recipes. Shellie and Chrys share from their personal grand journeys, and the stories they share are sweet, life-giving, and at times challenging.

But I know this: I'm encouraged to lean more into my grandparent time—it is so sweet and life-giving (and I don't have to be the rule enforcer—that's Mom and Dad's job!). This book will delight, inspire and encourage you—don't miss it.

MARY R SNYDER, Compassion International, virtual events team

As the Honey of seven grand darlings—ranging from newborn to teenager—myself, I appreciate Chrys and Shellie's sound wisdom from God's Word, seasoned with years of life experience as grandmothers themselves. From start to finish, this book is full of wit, humor, practical advice, and my personal favorite—tried and true recipes from a sisterhood of fellow grandmas that are guaranteed to be a blessing to your grandkids. I was encouraged on every page and reminded of the incredible privilege, honor, and responsibility I've been given to help shape and influence the next generation for His glory!

STEPHANIE "HONEY" HOLDEN, pastor's wife and storyteller

ROCKING IT GRAND

Rocking It
GRAND

— 18 WAYS TO BE A —
GAME-CHANGING GRANDMA

Chrys Howard and
Shellie Rushing Tomlinson

FOCUS
ON THE FAMILY.

A Focus on the Family Resource
Published by Tyndale House Publishers

Dedication

I'm dedicating this book to my sweet grandchildren who challenge me to be the best I can be. Thank you, sweet grands, for the privilege of loving you and sharing life with you. In my quest to be a game-changing grandma, you are the real game-changers! Making each day shine so much brighter anytime you call, text, Snapchat, direct message, FaceTime, or—the best—come over to see me! I love you to the moon and back and can't wait for the next generation of great-grands to join our big family.

HUGS, 2-MAMA (CHRYS)

◌◠◌

What a blessing it is to dedicate my share of these words to my grands, The Super Six. You wreck my heart in the best of ways, and experiencing life through your eyes is the gift that keeps on giving. You remind me just how important it is to laugh hard, play harder, and truly see our Father's world as it unfolds around us. Life with you makes me a better person. Here's to more grand adventures! To borrow the phrasing of C. S. Lewis, my deepest desire for you and for me is that we begin to know God and never finish.

HUGS, KEGGIE (SHELLIE)

Contents

Introduction *xiii*

1. Our Ceiling Is Their Floor *1*
2. Benchwarmers Make Valuable Players *11*
3. They Don't Want to Entertain Us *21*
4. Not All Castles Are the Same *31*
5. Listening Is the Secret to Being Heard *39*
6. Blend Until There Are No Lumps *49*
7. Little Ones Understand More Than We Think *59*
8. Their Thoughts Are Worth More than a Penny *69*
9. Teach Them to Stand *79*
10. Little Things Are Valuable *89*
11. In Our Weakness, Grandkids Grow Stronger *99*
12. Lead Them to Jesus by Going First *107*
13. The Puzzle's Corners Keep It Together *117*
14. Make the Best of Bad Situations *125*
15. Things That Matter Take Hard Work *135*
16. Experience Is Worth More than Advice *143*
17. Living in the Present Is a Gift *155*
18. Superheroes Don't Always Wear Capes *165*

Acknowledgments *177*
Index of Cookie Recipes *179*
About the Authors *181*

Introduction

*W*elcome to *Rocking It Grand*! If you've found this book, you're either a new grandma or already have a few little cuties who love you unconditionally and call you one of the many nontraditional grandma names floating around today. Chrys is called "2-mama" by her grands and Shellie is called "Keggie" by hers. We love our names and wouldn't trade them for the world, and we're sure you love yours, too.

So are we rocking this grandma thing? Absolutely! And we love keeping up on social media with our grandma friends as they post and boast about their grands. It's the one thing the world can agree on—grandkids add sparkle to any day, even if they're not your grandchildren. But yours are the best. Right?

As much as we love our grands and need them in our lives, guess what? They need us, too. Not just for an occasional cookie or the lollipop you hide in your purse for bribing purposes, but because we fill their love tanks. A grandma is the one person capable of taking over when Mom can't be there. Even if Mom is in the same room, a hurting child just might turn to Grandma because no one hugs, soothes, and comforts better than she can.

You might be thinking, *What are the rules for being a grandma today? It seems like things have changed since my days as a grandchild. I'm not anything like my grandma. Plus, things have changed since my kids were little. What does a grandma in today's world look like?*

We don't have all the answers, but we have some! And we would love to go on this amazing grandma journey with you as, together, we hone our grandma skills.

We've used Scripture, quotes, and our own personal stories to help you understand just how valuable grandmas can be! We have the potential to be game-changers, but to do so, we must be intentional. It won't happen accidentally. It can be tempting to step aside and play a lesser role because we've raised our children, but we want to challenge all of us to step up and into this grandma life, in the way God intends for one generation to mentor the next. God designed us in such a way that our influence is needed to help raise godly young men and women. Often stepping into such an important role can bring doubts and worries, but trust us when we say that you've got this because God's got you! So rock on, Grandma!

As a bonus, we've included twenty cookie recipes from the rocking grandmas in our families. You'll find our contributions as you turn the page. We know that some days just call for a good cookie. Isn't that right, Grandma?

Hugs to all you "rocking" grandmas.
Chrys and Shellie

2-mama's Famous B-52s

This is a family favorite that Chrys started making in her early twenties. She believes the original name was I-45s, but when she took it to a family gathering for the first time, someone asked her the name and she couldn't remember it. So she said B-52s. That's been the name ever since. Whatever it's called, it's a favorite. Enjoy!

INGREDIENTS:

 1 stick of butter, melted
 1 egg, beaten
 1 box yellow cake mix
 1 8-ounce package of cream cheese, softened
 2 eggs, beaten
 1 cup brown sugar, packed
 1 cup confectioners' sugar, unsifted
 1 teaspoon vanilla extract
 1 pinch of salt

DIRECTIONS:

Preheat oven to 325°F. Combine melted butter, 1 egg, and cake mix. Spread into the bottom of a 9" x 13" pan, forming a small edge around the sides. Combine cream cheese, 2 eggs, brown sugar, confectioners' sugar, vanilla, and salt. Beat until smooth. Spread over cake mixture. (Here's where that edge you formed helps hold in the cream cheese mixture.) Bake at 325°F for 45 minutes. When done, sprinkle with confectioners' sugar (because it's not sweet enough!). Let cool. Cut into squares.

> *Baking cookies is comforting, and cookies are the sweetest little bit of comfort food. They are very bite-sized and personal.*
>
> —— SANDRA LEE ——
> TV HOST, FOOD AND LIFESTYLE AUTHOR, AND
> CONTRIBUTOR FOR *Good Morning America*

Keggie's Amazing Chocolate Caramel Cookies

This is as near to perfect as a cookie can get. It'll bake to a nice crunch around the edges, while maintaining a chewy center, thanks to those caramel pieces. Keggie says trust her. You'll score big points with these cookies!

INGREDIENTS:

    1 cup (2 sticks) salted butter, softened
    1 cup granulated sugar
    1 cup brown sugar, packed
    2 eggs
    2 teaspoons vanilla extract
    2¾ cups (12 ounces) all-purpose flour
    ¾ teaspoon coarse sea salt

1 teaspoon baking soda
1½ teaspoons baking powder
1½ cups semi-sweet chocolate chips
1½ cups caramel chips

DIRECTIONS:

Preheat oven to 350°F. Cream softened butter with sugars. Blend about 2 minutes until the batter is fluffy, and then add eggs and vanilla extract. Continue blending another couple of minutes. Add baking soda, baking powder, and salt. Slowly add flour until it's incorporated into the batter. This last step will deliver the chocolate bang and the chewy caramel flavor: Add semisweet chocolate chips and caramel chips! Drop 1½ tablespoons of batter per cookie on a cookie sheet and bake 14 to 16 minutes. Closely watch your cookies because all ovens vary. Your cookies are ready when the edges are golden brown. Allow the cookies to cool a couple of minutes on the cookie sheet—if you can.

A balanced diet is a cookie in each hand.

BARBARA JOHNSON
AUTHOR AND WOMEN OF FAITH SPEAKER EMERITUS

Our Ceiling
Is Their Floor

A few years ago, I (Chrys) traveled with my granddaughter Sadie Robertson to one of her speaking appearances. While there, I ran into a young lady who had attended a church in our small town and knew our family. She asked if she could bless me and pray over me. Her words touched my heart in a profound way. She said that the hard work my husband and I had done in the Kingdom of God would be the foundation for our children and grandchildren to serve the Lord. Then she said, "Your ceiling will be the floor for the lives of your grandchildren." Wow! What an inspiring thought! All the things we had worked for, prayed about, strived to achieve, aimed to do, conquered, cried over, and fought for become the floor—the foundation—for our grandchildren to build upon!

It was such a powerful blessing, especially on that day, since I was with my granddaughter who was about to speak to a group of teens about her faith. My granddaughter is so much more than I was at eighteen years old. She passed me up in spiritual growth and now speaks to thousands of young people about Jesus. She's also been on a national dance competition show where she proudly and boldly shone the light on Jesus. Is Sadie able to do all of those things so comfortably and confidently because she's standing on the spiritual floor built by her parents, grandparents, and great-grandparents?

I saw this concept come to life in 2017 when my husband, Johnny, and I decided to take our entire family to Israel for a tour of the Holy Land. It was such a blessing to walk where Jesus walked with my kids and grandkids. None of us will ever forget our trip. One of the most profound places we visited was in Jerusalem. There we stood gazing into a giant hole. In that deep hole, people can view the remnants of three different civilizations—one on top of another. What this young lady at Sadie's speaking engagement had prayed over me I was now seeing in real life. One civilization was built on top of another. Centuries came and went. As each generation (or civilization) worked and toiled to build their lives, they set the stage for the next generation to continue the work. Years of excavating now give us a clear picture of how one civilization's ceiling became the floor of another.

But how does this work with *spiritual* ceilings and floors?

I have no idea what my great-grandparents did on a day-to-day basis, but I do know that they loved God. I'm fairly confident they didn't attend anything that resembled a major Christian youth rally like the event I attended with Sadie. I can also say with confidence that they didn't attend a summer camp where they played games and swam in a big pool. No, these events didn't exist in their time. But I'm sure they attended church, fed the hungry, cared for the sick, and went to the church potluck. I know they tucked their kids into bed at night and prayed over them.

You see, the layers of spiritual civilizations will look as different as the layers of physical civilizations. As a society and as individuals we grow and change; our methods will change even when the message does not. Just as every civilization cooks and cares for their families, each in a different way, every civilization seeks God in a distinct manner. While I can't dig a hole to see the layers of God's Word lived out in the lives of my ancestors, I know it happened. I heard the stories and am a recipient of their good deeds.

Here's one example: My husband's dad, Alton Howard, founded a Christian camp in 1967. His vision was to create a place where young people could learn more about God and each other while being outside in nature. He bought a hundred acres in West Monroe, Louisiana, and the dream began. Now more than fifty years later, his great-grandson, John Luke Robertson, is the director of that camp. Papaw Howard had no idea his great-grandson would one day take over the camp's operations, but he would be happy to know it. Papaw laid the foundation, my husband and I kept it going, and now John Luke is growing it into the future.

Recently, I was blessed to participate in a podcast with my mother, Jo, one of my daughters, Korie, and one of my granddaughters, Bella. Four of our five generations were represented in this podcast about legacy. We were asked to share one thing that we valued and had handed down to our children. Since Bella was the youngest and didn't have children, she planned to share something that had been passed on to her. Yet all of us—even my mother, who is ninety at the time I write this—shared what had been handed down to us. Then we talked about the values we wanted to pass on to others. We had assumed only Bella would share what had been handed down to her. But we discovered that we couldn't share what we'd passed along to our own children until we talked about what we ourselves had received. That's legacy living. That's leaving a ceiling strong enough to carry the weight of your children and grandchildren and supportive enough to inspire more growth in the future generation.

As we contemplate our legacies, one thing we must consider is how we'll confidently hand over the reins to our children and grandchildren. My daddy was a wise man; he always told me that no one is irreplaceable.

In our lifetimes, we've seen talented men and women come and go. They had remarkable, brilliant minds like Steve Jobs; unforgettable acting skills like John Wayne; comedic genius like Robin Williams; amazing voices like Whitney Houston, and on and on. Each of these men and women held a place in this world big enough that many people wondered if they could be replaced. But then someone did. New voices, new ideas, new jokes—something new replaces what we thought was irreplaceable. And over and over, we hear of young men and women who credit one of the people I mentioned above with laying a foundation for them to grow. They raised up a ceiling that became the floor for others to build upon.

Ecclesiastes says, "For everything there is a season" (Ecclesiastes 3:1), and God designed us for a specific time and place. Each of us will take our turns at being a child and a teenager, and many of us will become moms and dads and grandparents. It's the circle of life that is so beautifully displayed in the movie and play *The Lion King*. It's glorious to be part of a moment when you *realize* the legacy is being passed on.

Yet many of us feel confused and uncertain about our purpose as we reach this new stage of life. That's natural. After pouring our hearts, souls, and everything else into raising our kiddos, it's no wonder it takes us a while to find a new purpose. When the grandbabies start arriving, we think, *You've got this. This is familiar territory. It will all come back. It's like riding a bike.* But when it's your turn to babysit, the new mom shows up with a video baby monitor (which we never had), a heart monitor to strap on the baby's foot (which we never had), a huge blanket and instructions to "swaddle the baby" (which we never did), and a sound machine (which we never had). That's when we begin to let thoughts swirl around in our heads: *You're out of sync with the world. You don't know what you're doing. You don't have anything to offer.*

We're here to tell you *none of that is true!*

Just because times change doesn't mean your purpose has changed. In fact, your purpose just became more valuable. In Proverbs 13:22, King Solomon wrote: "A good man leaves an inheritance to his children's children." He's talking about your grandchildren—your children's children. King Solomon, who was the wisest man in the world, saw how important we, the grandparents, are in the lives of our grandchildren.

But what kind of inheritance is Solomon talking about? When I listened to eighteen-year-old Bella share on the podcast that she loved her family because they encouraged her to be anything she wanted to be and not feel tied to her hometown, I knew. Solomon wasn't talking about leaving a financial inheritance. He was talking about leaving our grandchildren values, attitudes, attributes, and character traits that will catapult them into adulthood with confidence and strength. I had three children to mentor, shape, and mold. I have fourteen grands and five great-grandchildren, so far. My job hasn't gone away—it's multiplied! It's the same for you. As long as we're on this earth, we're to keep aiming high and fortifying our ceilings so our children's children will have foolproof floors, foolproof foundations.

I love the song "The Blessing" performed by Kari Jobe and Cody Carnes. The lyrics speak of God's favor resting upon the generations, from parents to their children and then to their grandchildren.

In your grandparenting role, you are no less important

than you have been at any time in your life. Your children and their children and their children are all counting on you. It's your turn to be the tried, true, and tested one. It's your turn to pass wisdom, experience, and capability on to the next generation.

Our future generations depend on you and me! Let's raise the bar high!

Hugs,
Chrys

Reflect on It

ALL GOOD MEN AND WOMEN MUST TAKE RESPONSIBILITY TO CREATE LEGACIES THAT WILL TAKE THE NEXT GENERATION TO A LEVEL WE COULD ONLY IMAGINE.

JIM ROHN, AMERICAN BUSINESSMAN AND AUTHOR

If you don't have the generational legacy of faith that I have, it can start with you. If you have grandchildren, you're already the generational leader of your family. I once read that grandchildren are not able to picture their grandparents as young men and women. On some levels that's a sad reality, but on other levels, it's a blessing. Our grandchildren have the opportunity to experience the best of us. While we're not perfect, we've lived through many adventures. Share those adventures with your grands. Teach them through your stories and allow them to see you today as a woman of integrity.

After you're gone, how you lived your life will help them make life decisions with more confidence. They will surely ask themselves, *What would grandma (or grandpa) do?*

Remember It

We will not hide them from their children,
 but tell to the coming generation
the glorious deeds of the LORD, and his might,
 and the wonders that he has done.

PSALM 78:4

Rock It

Discovering your genealogy has never been easier. Track down some of your ancestry, and then write it down for your kids and grands. Because I've done this, I walked into a Mississippi museum and recognized the name of an Indian chief! He was a cousin of an ancestor who was also a Choctaw Indian chief. Give your kids and grandkids a brief history lesson about those who walked before them.

K-mama's Haystack Cookies

K-mama is Korie Robertson's grandma name. Korie is Chrys's daughter. This is the perfect fall cookie and one Korie made often when her kids were little. It's easy to make and fun to eat.

INGREDIENTS:

- 6 ounces butterscotch chips
- 6 ounces peanut butter chips
- 3 tablespoons peanut butter (regular, not all-natural or chunky)
- 1 package (6 ounces) dry chow mein noodles

DIRECTIONS:

Line a baking sheet with parchment paper. In a large bowl, combine the butterscotch chips, peanut butter chips, and peanut butter. Microwave on 50% power in 30-second intervals until the chips begin to lose their shape. Stir until melted and smooth. Quickly fold in the chow mein noodles with a large rubber spatula. While the mixture is still warm, form into small mounds (about 2 inches wide and 2 inches tall) on the lined baking sheet. Let sit at room temperature until firm. Store in an airtight container at room temperature.

A grandma's cookie jar can never be too full.

— KAY ROBERTSON —

2

Benchwarmers Make Valuable Players

*N*ever underestimate the value of a strong bench. This sports-loving grandma (Shellie) watched the scenario play out from the bleachers too many times over the years not to notice, and I saw it up close and personal during my years of coaching girls' basketball. I'm talking about the power of a substitute to reignite the first string and change the outcome of the game.

Take the role of a defensive specialist. In basketball lingo, that term refers to someone with the ability to shut down offensive opponents, hindering their scoring ability. I coached bench players who might not be able to hit the side of a barn with a basketball, but if they could frustrate an opposing player with a hot hand, they earned themselves playing time. However, I discovered in my coaching years that it wasn't always the offensive or defensive skills of the person called in for reinforcements that changed the momentum for our team, and sometimes it wasn't the person's sorely needed fresh legs that saved the day. There were many times when it was the substitute's attitude alone that lifted the other players' spirits and made all the difference in the game. Encouragement is contagious.

Substitutes come into the game with a unique perspective. While the weary warriors have been simply trying to keep their wits about themselves in the heat of battle, enthusiastic teammates coming off the bench have a distinct advantage. Because they've been watching the situation with cooler heads, they can often see what needs to be done to break up an offensive or defensive pattern that's threatening to wreak havoc on the team's short-term strategy and long-term goals. They not only bring fresh legs into the game but also bring fresh perspective!

This is the type of potential we grandparents have when our kids are straining under the nonstop demands of caring for the daily needs of our grands. We remember those days. We know what it's like to keep growing bellies fed and little bodies clothed, leaving zero time for self-care. Game-changing grandmas can use that experience to shore up the first string (the parents). With a few well-chosen and timely words, you and I can bring fresh energy to the situation, and we don't have to wait for the coach to call our cell phone number.

My husband and I share an ongoing group text with our grown children and their spouses that is perfectly suited for these benchwarmer moments. The grands aren't included in these family threads. They're too young right now, but I feel sure they'll take part one day. I'm looking forward to that. I see growing promise in these group messages to help strengthen the home team!

For the most part, we use our group conversations to communicate important information about upcoming family gatherings, scheduling updates, and who was the star at basketball, softball, or soccer practice. Sometimes our messages may be about who learned to go potty and who lost another tooth. (As of this writing, those two admirable feats have all been accomplished by the grandchildren, but hey, you never know.) I make it a point not to blow up the family thread with random observations, but occasionally I simply have to hijack it for something I jokingly refer to as "Drive-by Preaching." It's my way of seizing this fabulous technological opportunity to encourage the first string and strengthen our family game. Not long ago I had a sudden burst of insight and a handy smartphone. Bless my people's hearts, it was a combination I couldn't resist.

"Excuse the intrusion," I typed to the group, "but I've got to tell y'all what I'm thinking about because it was so strong in my prayer time this morning."

With that warning, I jumped into my message. I reminded my people that God chose us through Christ Jesus. It's true that we have to choose Him back, I told them, but God chose us first. I figured they were thinking, *We know that, Keggie. And we're kind of busy here.* So before they could respond I cut them off at the pass. It's what we Drive-by Preachers do.

"I realize y'all know this," I typed out, "but stay with me for a minute. Have you ever considered that we are always choosing Him—or not choosing Him? This is where the potential lies to transform our lives, and it's enormous. I believe that long after our initial response, God waits for us to choose Him again, and again, and again, day after day after day. He wants us to choose Him in this present moment and in the next one, to choose to hold Him in our thoughts over the noise of everything going on around us. He made us capable of choosing to be conscious of Him in the thick of it! I don't understand it, but I know there's power in these choices of ours that can change our todays and our tomorrows. When we choose Him, He refreshes us wherever we are and strengthens us in whatever challenges we're facing!"

Then, before I sent them off with a "that's all, folks," I hit 'em with my big finish: "For remember, it's never His Presence that we lose, it's only the sense of His Presence. Let's choose Him today, all day."

Based on the feedback, my morning missive was timely encouragement for our first-string players to turn to God and draw fresh supplies for their parenting game. I didn't even get penalized for the lengthy texting! I suppose that kind of response would be music to any grandma's ears. I know it certainly blessed mine.

I understand that my busy kids might need a reminder to ask for heavenly reinforcements, because this Keggie also needs remedial prompts to quit trying to do life under her own steam. I love to remind my independent and goal-oriented daughter that the first words to come out of her little mouth were "Me do it!" But I think we're all inclined toward a "me do it" mindset. We find it easier to fall back into the default habit of drawing on our own limited human resources rather than stopping to call out to our ever-present Father. Our nerves might be frayed and our determination flagging, but we'll suck it up and play on like it's all up to us to win the day. Friends, there are no points awarded for this type of stubbornness. On the contrary, it costs us, and it costs those we love.

Why? Because relying on our own get-it-done mentalities means we forfeit the privilege of drawing from our Father's unlimited resources of additional supplies that include wisdom, patience, and strength. We're never penalized for asking Jesus for more resources! On the contrary, over and again, Jesus urges us to "come unto me"! It's His invitation when we first come to believe, and it's His ongoing encouragement. It's not easy to remember to call a time-out and request holy help when we're used to knuckling down and gritting our way through life's challenges, but I've discovered God is willing to help us form this type of new and powerful habit. Let's ask Him to prompt us and then revel in His faithfulness!

Experiencing God's willingness to engage with us in what

we consider the inconsequential, mundane routines of life is reason enough to call to Him, but there's an added incentive for those of us who aim to be game-changing grandmas. When we make it our practice to draw from the well that never runs dry, we're able to share the treasure with our loved ones! We get to teach them where to go for lasting help. We're privileged to model a life for our kids and our grandchildren that helps them discover the joy of walking with God and experiencing His faithful presence in their own everyday lives.

By the way, whether you're responding to a direct call to action or feeling a sudden urge to prop up your home team with some Drive-by Preaching, I've got a tip for you. Experience has taught me that it helps when we talk *with* our tired teammates instead of talking *at* them. We increase our effectiveness by acknowledging that we need the information we're passing along as much as they do! The more we lose the "you should" suggestions for more "let's remember" encouragements, the better chance we have of being heard. We had our opportunities to teach our kids when they were young. Those days are gone, and the game has changed. Let's change with it by modeling a life of continued learning and growing right along with them. The first string will benefit the most from our pep talk when we recognize our need to hear it too!

Hugs,
Shellie

Reflect on It

SO TO ALL THE BENCHWARMERS OUT THERE: RIDE THE PINE WITH PRIDE AND BE PATIENT. YOUR MOMENT OF GLORY IS COMING.

JUSTIN SCANSON

As a team member comes off the court or playing field, those on the sidelines (the benchwarmers) will often line up and greet them with a high five or a fist bump. It may seem like a small gesture, but the support it communicates can be greatly needed and appreciated. Likewise, with our kids and our grandkids, little words or signs of affirmation can be crucial to helping them feel as if the challenges they're facing can be conquered, especially if the encouragement comes at a moment when they may be feeling rattled and unsure of themselves. Whether it's a word, a smile, a hug, or a note in the mail, simple acts can say "I'm on your side" and "You've got this." These gestures are valuable far beyond the moment when they're offered. Never forget the power of a well-planned or spontaneous pat on the back. The dividends can be eternal.

Besides words, our actions as a grandparent show the first string (the parents) that we're ready to be in the game. Benchwarmers have to stay ready and alert, watching and observing, so that when they're called into the game, they can be of immediate help. Know your children's parenting techniques. Be mindful and stay away from actions that might undermine what they're doing as parents. If they restrict their kid's sugar intake, don't pass out candy on the sly! Be respectful of their decisions and carry them out as best you can. Being called in to "take over" means they value you and know you'll do an amazing job. Go for it, Grandma. Sit on that bench with your head held high and your heart ready for action!

Remember It

Therefore encourage one another and build one another up, just as you are doing.

I THESSALONIANS 5:11

Rock It

Even if you're not called off the bench this week, encourage your family members with words that will inspire their efforts and strengthen their resolve. Be intentional about choosing God and spending time in His Word and in prayer, and you'll always have game-changing refreshments on hand for others.

Nana Faubion's Everything Cookies

Nana is Shellie's middle sister, Rhonda. She's been making these sweets long before she had grands, but her favorite littles agree with the rest of the family—these cookies are everything!

INGREDIENTS:

1 cup melted margarine
1 cup vegetable oil
2 cups brown sugar, packed
2 cups granulated sugar
1 cup coconut flakes
1 6-ounce bag semisweet chocolate chips
1 6-ounce bag milk chocolate chips
4 beaten eggs
2 teaspoons vanilla extract
2 cups oatmeal
2 cups cornflakes
4 cups all-purpose flour
2 teaspoons baking soda
2 teaspoons baking powder

DIRECTIONS:

Preheat oven to 350°F. Combine all ingredients and mix well. Drop by teaspoonfuls onto greased cookie sheets and bake 7 to 8 minutes. Tip: Nana chills her dough before baking!

> *When you're down and feeling worse,*
> *keep a cookie in your purse.*
> — ANONYMOUS

3

They Don't Want to
Entertain Us

I could hear my grand-girls in the guest room changing into their pj's and preparing for bed. The sound of their laughter blessed me as it trickled down the hall to the master bedroom where I was hanging up the last of my laundry. Their loud giggles suggested it might be a while before the Sandman actually visited. I made a mental note to see if the girls even knew about the Sandman. I haven't heard anyone mention the Sandman in ages, but as a kid I was fascinated by the idea of a stranger who was accused of getting children to go to sleep by putting magical sand in their eyes! You must admit, it's a strange fable.

I was about to turn off the light when something shiny

caught my eye. It was those too-tight-for-my-feet-but-super-cute boots I'd bought on sale. They were a fashionable silvery bronze with just the right-sized heel, and they'd already proven to be all kinds of adorable with dressy jeans. Unfortunately, they'd also given me painful blisters. I suspected they were sized wrong. Bummer. (In the interest of full disclosure, I knew they were too snug when I bought them, but did I mention they were on sale and super cute? I suspect you understand that reasoning.)

It occurred to me that the grand-girls might be able to wear them. I wanted to dismiss the thought! Weren't these kids in high chairs only last week? They couldn't possibly be ready for silvery-bronze heels! Then again, we'd just finished a spa night complete with facials and manicures. Reality check in one hand and cute shoes in the other, I headed to the girls' bedroom.

"Hey girls, do either of you want to try on these new shoes? They're too tight for me."

I wasn't surprised when the girls both voiced an interest in the boots, but I couldn't believe my eyes when the footwear fit their sweet feet like Cinderella's slipper—both of them, big sis and little sis too! Oh, say it ain't so. The grand-girls and I can now swap shoes? When did this happen? I knew the oldest grandson's foot had outgrown mine, but the bellerinas? I understand if you aren't familiar with the term. I coined the word *bellerina* for my readers when the girls were born. ***Bellerina (bell-er-een-a), noun: tiny female of the Southern persuasion.***

Have mercy. The bellerinas have officially outgrown their name.

It happens, right? We know this. Our kids grew up right before our eyes, and these precious grands of ours will too. It's warp speed, all of it. We can't change it, Grandma, but we can prepare for it! And there's a bonus here for those who do. If we're intentional about preparing for it, the changing seasons lying straight ahead can nourish our family bonds instead of stressing them.

The question is, how do we prepare for all of this growing and changing before our very eyes? I don't pretend to have all the answers, but here's one. We prepare for it by holding on to our own lives while we celebrate theirs! Spending time with the grands is great fun, and showing up for their sports and school activities blesses both sides, but game-changing grandmas resist the urge to let their entire world be swallowed up in their grands' lives. However charming their worlds might be, it's wise to realize that it's not healthy for all of our days to be centered exclusively on the next babysitting opportunity or Little League game. The key word here being *exclusively*. We're setting ourselves up for future disappointment when we don't continue pursuing our own interests and hobbies and nurturing our marriages and friendships even as we "ooh and aah" over these little people who hold our hearts in their itty-bitty hands. Otherwise, we won't know what to do with ourselves when we're no longer on active grand duty and our days are ours to fill again.

You know that day is coming too, right? That's another

reality check we need to confront. Tricycles and nap times will soon give way to braces and brand-new drivers with permits in their eager, teenage hands. With those wheels come new experiences and increasing independence. Translation? I don't like writing it any more than you enjoy reading it, but our homes won't always be their favorite destinations. And one day—brace yourself—they may just prefer their friends' company to yours.

I'll never forget the first time my oldest grandchild waved at me from a distance because she was running with a group of her friends and was too busy to stop for Keggie love! *Wait! What was this? A flyby from my huggy-buddy?* I was not a fan of this development. I'd been used to bracing myself as she headed toward me for a hug like an out-of-control mini-linebacker bent on taking down the other team's quarterback. Did my heart break just a little? Oh, yes, it did. But I took my own advice, swallowed hard, and reminded myself it was a natural progression. It's more than that, though. It's actually a good thing! That's right, a good thing. Hear me out, Grandma.

This growing independence that feels too much like separation is what we want for them. The challenge is to stop moaning in our coffee long enough to realize it. We've done our job, and we've done it well. We've given our kids and grandkids the life skills they need to begin venturing out into the world without us and pursuing their own God-given purposes in this life. We should give ourselves a high five! They'll still love us, and they'll still need us, just in a different way.

It won't be as hands-on as it is when they're little, but every stage brings new ways to interact with them, and we can be confident the bonds we created with them in their childhood years will be there as a firm foundation for the rest of their lives. One of the worst things we can do if we want healthy relationships with our grands is to make them feel guilty for growing up! Clinging rarely brings anyone closer, and it usually pushes people away.

What I'm urging us to remember is that we put undue strain on any relationship when we place a human in the position of being our "everything" and look for that person to meet all of our emotional needs. We also invite conflict if we expect anyone else to help us fill our days with activities, and that includes those who dearly love us. Eventually that sort of dependency becomes an unhealthy situation for all involved. Neither our kids nor our grandkids can carry the full weight of our need for social interaction or entertainment, and we shouldn't expect them to try. If our goal is to stay relevant in their lives, we must be careful not to make our loved ones feel guilty when their days don't always include us. Not only does that expectation apply too much pressure, but our grandkids may also come to resent us for it. Isn't that the last thing we want?

If you're thinking this is all easier said than done, let me be quick to admit that I get it. I do! It's why I say we have to be intentional about creating family dynamics that let one another breathe and grow. If we're going to avoid this emotional hotbed, we need to be making plans that address it, and that brings me back to those hobbies and interests we talked about earlier.

Think about it this way: Continuing to explore the world around us and develop as persons in our own right is a gift to our loved ones. It's an investment in our present and our future relationships. Why? Because pursuing our own interests has the added benefit of making us more interesting people, and that in itself makes others want to spend time with us! Now that's what I call a win-win.

Hugs,
Shellie

Reflect on It

AS GOD IS EXALTED TO THE RIGHT PLACE IN OUR LIVES,
A THOUSAND PROBLEMS ARE SOLVED ALL AT ONCE.

A. W. TOZER, CHRISTIAN PASTOR AND AUTHOR

Living in a celebrity culture, we've all seen shooting stars crash and burn. We've had ringside seats to the carnage that comes from treating humans like gods. I imagine we all probably thought of at least one person when we read those words. Someone once said we build them up to watch them fall. Sadly, it rings true. Man was created to worship, not to be worshiped, and flipping the formula invites disaster in the red-carpet world. We know that, but we can be slower to realize that it also creates havoc in our family circles. We're meant to love our children and grandchildren, but they aren't meant to be our "everything," and they don't need to be our reason for living. God not only demands that spot, but He knows that loving Him above everyone else is in our best interest, and theirs.

Bottom line? Let's love on these precious grands, spoil 'em a little (or a lot!), and see them as often as we can. Let's be present for as many activities as possible and take every opportunity to build memories with them. But let's also hold on to old hobbies and develop new ones. Were you a crafter once upon a time? There are so many more materials available to crafters than you and I could have ever imagined back in the day. Sites such as Pinterest abound with free ideas. Get an account and explore!

Perhaps you could take that growing collection of grandchild photos living on your smartphone and learn how to create interesting photo books. You could build books around different themes; for example, your grandkids' sports activities, cooking efforts, or musical endeavors. These make awesome gifts, as well, that any mom or grandchild would treasure!

Do you love to travel but the budget doesn't? You can take a virtual tour of the most famous sites in the world through online museums. Make a bucket list of things you've never seen and google it, Grandma! Form a Bible study with your peers. Schedule a regular walk with a neighbor. Whatever it is, let's read, learn, grow, and keep in mind that God alone can deal with the pressure of being our "everything." What's more, the Word says He welcomes it!

Remember It

> [Jesus] said to him, "You shall love the Lord your
> God with all your heart and with all your soul and
> with all your mind."
>
> MATTHEW 22:37

Rock It

Type the word *hobby* into the search bar at Pinterest.com and
find something that interests you! Warning, you may spend
more time there than you intended!

Grandmama Debbie's Birthday Cookie Cake

Debbie is Shellie's sister-in-law. We love cookie cakes, and
Grandmama Debbie offers a quick recipe to delight party-
goers of all ages! You'll score extra points with the grands if
they get to decorate.

INGREDIENTS:

2¼ cups all-purpose flour
1 teaspoon baking soda
1 teaspoon salt
1 cup (two sticks) butter, softened
¾ cup granulated sugar
¾ cup brown sugar, packed

1 teaspoon vanilla extract
2 large eggs
2 cups chocolate chips

DIRECTIONS:

Preheat oven to 350°F. Combine flour, baking soda, and salt in a small bowl. Beat butter, sugars, and vanilla extract in large bowl until creamy. Add eggs, one at a time, beating well after each egg. Gradually stir in flour mixture. Stir in chocolate chips. Press dough into a pizza pan that you've greased and floured. Spread evenly. Bake 15 to 20 minutes. Cool and decorate as desired.

> *I'm a picky eater. By that I mean I love to pick the raisins out of oatmeal raisin cookies, the chips out of chocolate chip cookies, the white side off of black and white cookies, and the vanilla center out of Oreos.*
>
> — DYLAN LAUREN —
> FOUNDER AND CEO OF DYLAN'S CANDY BAR

$$\left(\begin{array}{c}4\end{array}\right)$$

Not All Castles
Are the Same

$\mathcal{I}$n 2009 my husband and I (Chrys) were blessed to spend three months at Oxford University in England. At that point, it had been nearly forty years since we'd lived away from family. Even though it was just three months, I missed my family terribly. Still, it was an amazing time of adventure and discovery.

Much of our time was spent exploring castles in both England and Scotland. Magnificent castles with centuries of history grace the countrysides of most European countries. With our comparatively short history in America, these are sights not experienced on our back roads. At best, we see antebellum homes that aren't more than two hundred years old. So, it was fascinating to see structures from the thirteenth century still in use. (I've remodeled my house three times, and it's not even forty years old!)

One castle we toured was Urquhart Castle in Scotland. Urquhart Castle sits majestically and peacefully beside Loch Ness (*loch* means "lake") where the famous Loch Ness Monster is said to live. Like the many other castles we visited, this one was surrounded by many years of bloodshed as people fought for control of land. "Castle remains" would best describe Urquhart Castle today, but the tourist organization did a fantastic job of reenacting the time period in an eight-minute video, so by the time we walked into the castle ruins we could visualize grand dinners as well as everyday life.

Romantic views aside, from what we saw during our castle visits, you wouldn't have wanted your family to live in one during medieval times. The castle was magnificent, but the battle to keep it in one's possession was grueling, at best.

During the Urquhart Castle's glory years, around one hundred people lived in the castle/fortress, as it took many to care for the lord and lady and one another. Bakers, cooks, seamstresses, stewards, horse handlers, doctors, and many more servants were required to maintain day-to-day castle life. As I stood at one end of it, I was reminded of life at the summer camp I direct—a self-contained village where people live and, most certainly, love each other. The castle's history tells us that there would be several hundreds of years where life was uneventful in Urquhart Castle, but then war would break out, destroying all that the previous generations had worked for. The last battle was in 1689.

Why all this talk about castles? By the end of our three-month journey I said, "Let's not go to another castle. They all look alike." Here's the deal: Those castles did resemble one another. They each had tall, fortified walls, a turret somewhere, and perhaps a bridge or moat. Even their backstories began to sound alike.

Yet within each stone wall lived a family who did their best to live and work together to create a safe environment. Each castle *was* different. While the structures looked similar, the dreams and goals of its occupants were not the same. Each castle was dependent on its lord and lady to shape how it functioned. The personalities and the likes and dislikes of each lord and lady varied.

You've heard the saying, "A man's home is his castle." The phrase stresses that people can do what they please in their own homes, as lords and ladies did during castle eras. As Americans, we value our homes and our right to be who we are in them. Each household can make its own decisions, rules, and boundaries.

When our children are married and begin to build their own castles, the lines might blur—just a little. We might become a little "judgy" that our daughter doesn't wash her sheets weekly like we did in our castle, or our son has decided he likes Miracle Whip now instead of real mayo because that's what his wife likes. It's the little things that we can be judgmental about, right?

My three children are married with lives of their own. Each is in charge of his or her own castle. And here's the odd thing: They're all so different. "Didn't you raise them the same?" you might ask. I thought I did, but my three little people grew up to be three very different big people.

Why? Because God created all of my children unique. Imagine that. The nerve of God to give me children with three totally different personalities! If you have more than one child, you understand this concept. Your kids have distinctive personalities too. If you're like me, you've questioned God a time or two. *(God, I am in over my head here. Help me know what to say and what to do. What I did the last time doesn't work with this child!)*

Grandma, your grandchildren need you to love and accept their parents just as they are, whether they now eat real mayo or Miracle Whip. They need to see your eyes light up with joy when you visit their castle. There is no room for criticism. No room for complaints. No room for comparisons. No room for condemnations. No room for choosing to visit one castle over the other.

We had our time of teaching and training. When our children lived in our castles, we taught and talked until we were blue in the face about important issues. We taught manners and social responsibility. We taught them to be obedient to God and to serve others. We taught them to treat others with kindness and to be generous with what they have. We showed them how to be hospitable. We pleaded our case for wearing seatbelts and helmets and to never swim alone.

It was the responsibility of the lord and lady of the castles of old to protect those in their castle. And we did it. We didn't have a moat and a drawbridge, but there were times we wished we did. When our children reach the age where they occupy their own castles, our job is to support them. It's time to be still and trust in what we've done and how we've equipped them. But it's not easy.

Those three months we spent in England were hard for me because I watched my family live life from a distance. But that's what life with adult children is like anyway, isn't it? We do "watch from a distance" since we probably don't live with them and, even if we do, we should approach our relationship as if we live at a distance. I live next door to one of my children, five miles from another, and seven hours from another. My behavior has to be "watch from a distance" even if my adult child lives next door.

Our children are not in this world to build castles that look exactly like our castles. Not in the furniture they choose, the floor plans they select, or their decisions about who washes the dishes or takes out the trash. It becomes our job to accept that this is their life, not ours.

As one of six kids, I watched my parents love and accept every castle that was created from their original fortress. I've watched my mom give advice, only when asked, about everything from how to burp a baby to whether one should use tile, wood, or carpet in a game room. My mom's decision not to speak up unless asked has nothing to do with her being soft-spoken, because she isn't at all. She's extremely opinionated. It has everything to do with her having respect for her adult children and their personal choices. I have to admit, I'm not sure I've done as good a job as she's done in this area, but I try.

I do know this: Our grands need us to be there for them and their parents with unconditional love and support. There's no room in our families for castle fighting. Leave that to the history books and go forward with flags of peace and love.

Hugs,
Chrys

Reflect on It

YES, LET GOD BE THE JUDGE.
YOUR JOB TODAY IS TO BE A WITNESS.

WARREN WIERSBE,
CHRISTIAN CLERGYMAN, BIBLE TEACHER, AND WRITER

There is no better time for memorizing this quote than when your children start to build their own lives. Our job is to show others who God is through our unconditional love and support. I know I haven't done this perfectly and you will not either. When mistakes are made, accept your part of the problem and do what it takes to right the wrong. That will be a lesson too. So many families spend years fighting about something or in silence over an issue even though the details now seem vague. The Scriptures make it clear that inasmuch as it depends on me, I need to keep the peace.

Remember It

Let the peace of Christ, to which you were indeed
called in one body, rule in your hearts; and be
thankful.

COLOSSIANS 3:15, NASB

Rock It

Sometimes we get in the habit of waiting for our children to
call us. It's not without reason, since we often don't want to
disturb their busy lives. Even so, today might be a good time
to call your children and let them know you love them. Tell
them you're proud of them and how they've created their
castles to surround their loved ones. If you're able, you might
just want to send them flowers.

Honey's Christmas Cookies

Honey is Chrys's sister Joneal Kirby. For many years, she has
treated the entire family to a cookie-decorating night just
before Christmas. It's a fun family tradition that brings out
the artist in all ages. Her recipe has stood the test of time.

INGREDIENTS:

½ cup butter (1 stick), softened
½ cup dark brown sugar, packed

2/3 cup light molasses
1 egg
1 teaspoon vanilla extract
1 teaspoon ginger
1 teaspoon cinnamon
4 cups all-purpose flour
4 teaspoons baking powder

ICING:

1 pound confectioners' sugar
2 egg whites
1 tablespoon lemon juice

DIRECTIONS:

Cream butter and brown sugar together. Add egg, molasses, vanilla, ginger, and cinnamon. Beat until fluffy. Mix flour and baking powder together. Sift into butter mixture gradually. Roll into a ball, wrap in wax paper, and refrigerate. Cut dough into four parts and roll out 1/8" thick on a floured board. Cut into shapes. Bake at 350°F for 8 to 10 minutes. Cool completely before decorating.

Icing: Mix the confectioners' sugar, egg whites, and lemon juice. Beat for a few minutes. Spread on cookies.

Cookies are made of butter and love.

— ANONYMOUS —

5

Listening Is the Secret to Being Heard

As soon as grandkids are old enough to talk, they begin asking questions—a lot of questions—and they lob those questions at us with a pace that can be tiring if not totally overwhelming. No news flash there. What isn't quite so obvious, however, is the potential of these seemingly nonstop inquiries. There's potential, that is, if you take time to engage the child who's asking the questions.

No, I (Shellie) do not have the patience of Job, and I'm not trying to push you over the edge, Grandma. We'll unpack the gold hidden in these questions in just a moment, and we'll see how they can position us to be relevant in our grands' lives for years to come.

But first I'll share a tip that can preserve our sanity in the early days of the Q&A game. It reminds us to breathe and to remember that not all questions are created equal.

I well remember the day I had a relationship-impacting epiphany about my first grandchild's endless interrogations. Emerson was an itty-bitty thing riding in my car. As was her custom, she was happily peppering me with questions about anything, everything, and nothing when I suddenly realized it wasn't the answers Emerson was interested in as much as it was the conversation! It came as such a relief when it dawned on me that Emerson didn't *really* want to know why the sky was blue. She simply enjoyed the back-and-forth of communicating. With that one realization, our Silly Question Game was born. I started it by answering Emerson's next couple of questions with totally nonsensical explanations. Emerson was puzzled by my responses at first, but she caught on quickly and was soon sold on the ridiculous dialogue. The Silly Question Game became one of our favorites pastimes. It went something like this:

"Keggie, why is the sky blue?"

"Because frogs like to hop."

"But Keggie, why do frogs like to hop?"

"Because turtles have shells."

"Why do turtles have shells, Keggie?"

"Because bees buzz."

I'll stop there. I think you see the pattern. Clearly, my answers had nothing whatsoever to do with Emerson's questions, but then again, logic was immaterial to our game.

Communication was everything, and the sillier the exchange, the more we enjoyed it. Our game was a win-win! Emerson was able to indulge her need for conversation, and I didn't have to figure out why elephants have long noses and rabbits have big ears! Emerson is now a preteen. As you might imagine, we no longer play the Silly Question Game, but she and I both enjoy reliving the memory. It's written into our story.

Conversations with Emerson and the grands who came after her have now changed. As you know, little ones' queries change as they mature. They begin to ask questions that can be just as hard to answer as "Why do elephants have long noses?" But the Silly Question Game won't work anymore.

I think we can all agree our grands ask questions we can't and shouldn't answer because the subject matter isn't age appropriate or it's just too difficult for them to understand. And there are also questions that only their parents should address. But let's be honest with ourselves. There are just as many other times when we put their questions off or give them a place-holding type of answer because we just don't have the energy to make an effort.

It's okay to agree with me. We can admit that growing kids can have twice the persistence in asking questions than we have patience in answering them, but the reward of staying engaged with grands can't be overstated. It's why I highly recommend stopping to ask God to replenish our strength whenever we find it flagging, be that in the midst of grand duty or not. Jesus is the well that never runs dry. As for me, I'm needy and I know it! I'm always asking the Lord to remind me when I'm trying to do anything in my own power, including grandparenting, and He is faithful to do just that.

But about those questions . . .

Little kids ask endless questions because there is so much about their world they simply don't know. They're refreshingly honest about their ignorance. (If only we big people could follow that example!) Our grands are always processing. They're curious about everything, and they turn to us because they believe we have the answers. Yet like everything else, this too shall pass.

Let's think about what that means. You and I won't always be our grands' go-to source for information. As they grow, so will their circles of influence. We realize this will happen, even if we don't relish the reality. We all know we're in a temporary season with our grandchildren. So are we taking advantage of it? Are we acting in ways now that will allow us to remain relevant in their lives later?

Do we want to have relationships with our grandkids that will cause them to listen to us later on when the complex subjects arise? If we do, then let's be sure we're talking *with them* during these days and not just talking *at them*. The goal is to create a culture of conversation while the questions and answers aren't nearly as crucial as they will be in the years to come.

I'm not saying it's necessary for anyone to play the Silly Question Game with their littles that Emerson and I once loved, although it's yours for the taking! It's vitally important, however, to recognize the conversational opportunities that come after those early years. The grade-school and middle-school exchanges allow us to build a foundational relationship that can keep communication open in the teen years and beyond when conversation doesn't flow as naturally between the generations. Conversely, not expending the emotional or mental energy to engage when the grands are eager to talk to us practically guarantees that they'll seek other company when they have the option.

Yes, Q&As can be tiring. Answering questions all day, every day can take its toll, and some of us are better with explanations than others. Full disclosure? Not long ago I heard my daughter-in-law respond to my eleven-year-old grand's question about the Electoral College with the clarity of a high-school civics teacher! I may have been tempted to skip the details on that one! You don't have to be a civics teacher, but whenever possible, be ready to have those fuller conversations. Let's turn the radios down, turn the TVs off, and close our laptops. Let's put away our smartphones and talk to our precious grands. What's more, let's challenge ourselves to ask our own questions in response to theirs and give them time to think through their answers!

It's heartbreaking to think about the price our children are paying for our collective attention spans (and they're getting shorter all the time). Stop and think about the times you've seen a child trying to find the right words while the busy adult he or she is talking to either gets distracted or supplies the little one's missing words because the grown-up is too impatient to wait. Maybe, like me, you've been that busy parent or grandparent. Ouch! We can choose a better response.

We can give our grands a great gift by letting them have time to formulate a sentence without feeling like a clock is ticking! We'll help them build confidence in expressing themselves when we allow them space to try.

Will we have to be intentional about giving the fuller response? Absolutely. The "just enough" reply will always be the easier one, and don't we all favor the path of least resistance? However, thinking through questions along with our miniature inquisitors and allowing an exchange sends them the message we most want them to hear: Their thoughts matter because they do, and they're worth our time and attention.

While these reminders to build the habit and rhythm of conversation into our families are simple enough, the yield from such intentional grandparenting can't be measured. With God's help, we can train ourselves to see the daily opportunities we have to invest in another generation and make good use of our time together in the everyday moments. If we aspire to leave lasting words in our grands' lives that will help them find and nourish a deep and growing faith in Jesus, we must live in a certain way *now*. We must remind ourselves that our grandchildren won't hear us later if we don't listen to them now. We can set ourselves up to be heard on the eternal things that truly matter by intentionally engaging today on the topics that don't seem important. There's a day ahead when we'll be oh-so-glad we did!

Hugs,
Shellie

Reflect on It

CONVERSATION IS THE LABORATORY
AND WORKSHOP OF THE STUDENT.

RALPH WALDO EMERSON, NINETEENTH-CENTURY AMERICAN POET

The benefits our grands will reap from these early conversations go beyond our own goals of staying relevant in their expanding circles. Learning how to express themselves can position them for future success in every area of life from marriage relationships to career paths. At the same time, because we're all different, communicating will always come easier for some than others. This is where we can step in with timely training.

Our son could hold a conversation with grown men from the time he was old enough to sit in their midst. If the subject was farming, hunting, or his favorite sports team, all the better. Grown-ups responded favorably to Phillip's wide-open personality. Our daughter found it much harder to talk to adults. I discovered I could help Jessica become more comfortable with these public encounters by giving her a couple of easy ground rules. I required her to make eye contact with the adult and respond to his or her initial greeting or question. She didn't have to ad-lib or elaborate, but she did have to speak. Mind you, Jessica escaped like Houdini once she completed these minimum requirements, but eventually she found such exchanges bearable. Today, she runs her own successful business and can more than hold her own in any type of social setting.

As game-changing grandmas, we can give our grandkids

a head start in learning to communicate. Just remember, our conversations with them are like mini training camps, positioning our loved ones for winning seasons!

Remember It

Do nothing from selfish ambition or conceit, but in humility count others more significant than yourselves. Let each of you look not only to his own interests, but also to the interests of others.

PHILIPPIANS 2:3-4

Rock It

Pique your grands' interest and reel them into conversation by talking about their parents' childhoods. Tell them a story about something their mom or dad used to do or say when they were young, and chances are you'll have their full attention!

Nina Karen's Snickerdoodles

Every grandma needs a snickerdoodle recipe in her toolbox. Nina Karen is Shellie's sister-in-law. She says you can make these buttery, sweet cookies as chewy or crispy as you like by adjusting the baking time! Either way, we're sure they'll disappear!

COOKIE INGREDIENTS:

1 cup shortening
1½ cups granulated sugar
2 eggs
2¾ cups self-rising flour
2 teaspoons cream of tartar
1 teaspoon baking soda
½ teaspoon salt

TOPPING INGREDIENTS:

4 tablespoons sugar
4 teaspoons cinnamon

DIRECTIONS:

Mix the shortening, sugar, and eggs. Sift together flour, cream of tartar, baking soda, and salt in a separate bowl. Gradually stir the flour mixture into the shortening mixture. Chill the dough before rolling walnut-size balls.

TOPPING:

Mix the sugar and cinnamon. Roll the balls of dough in this sugar mixture until they're well covered. Place on ungreased cookie sheets. Press down a little with a fork. Bake at 400°F for 8 to 10 minutes.

> *When the going gets tough,*
> *the tough make cookies.*
> — ERMA BOMBECK —
> AMERICAN HUMORIST

6

Blend Until There Are No Lumps

I'm definitely not the cook of the two people writing this book. But I (Chrys) do know this: Blending involves combining two or more ingredients until the end result is as smooth and combined as possible. As a full-time provider of food for my family, but a part-time cook, I also know some ingredients are more easily blended than others. (Personally, I still get lumps in my pancake batter, but I hear that's okay.) In any case, blending anything requires work.

My granddaughter Bella loves to cook. One day at my house she baked cookies using a recipe that had been handed down from an aunt who was born in 1907 and lived in a log cabin until she passed away in 1995. (See recipe at the end of this chapter.) The recipe called for eight cups of flour and three cups of sugar. That's a lot of dry ingredients! Then it called for butter and sour cream with instruction to "blend until smooth." Even though we used an electric hand mixer, Bella needed to get up on the kitchen counter to gain enough leverage to blend the ingredients together. It was quite a sight! At one point the electric mixer started smoking, and Bella had to mix by hand the rest of the way! Contrast that scene to me mixing the confectioners' sugar, butter, and milk to make a cookie glaze. Yep, I got the better of the two jobs. Clearly, some ingredients are just harder to work with!

The cookie-baking analogy pretty much describes relationships. One important lesson in life is realizing that some people and some circumstances make having a cohesive relationship more difficult. Some people require so much effort that you need to jump up on the counter and use every muscle in order for the relationship to work, while others will blend together as smoothly as confectioners' sugar and butter. But no matter how much work the blending process involves, God wants us to seek unity to further the gospel. And sometimes grandparents are called to aid in the blending process in their own families.

Consider the two ladies called out in Philippians 4. Euodia and Syntyche (how about those names?) are two prominent women in the church at Philippi. Paul urges them to think the same thing. There's some discussion among commentators as to what the "same thing" is, but it's clear that Paul knows these two sisters in the faith need to present a unified front to advance the gospel message. I also love that Paul asks others to help Euodia and Syntyche in their efforts to work together. This is not a call to cut down these two sisters; rather, it is a call to build them up in the faith they share.

As game-changing grandparents and, more importantly, believers in Christ, it's also our job to be unified in our message even when the circumstances are hard for us personally. In Euodia and Syntyche's case, we're not told the details surrounding the conflict, and I think God did that on purpose. It's human nature to want to place blame on one party or the other. We definitely do this with our children, don't we? The fight breaks out. We separate. Then we ask, "Who started this?" But Paul leaves out the details. I believe that's because the cause isn't as important as the cure. That's the truth with our kids, too, isn't it? I found with my own kids it was more beneficial in the long run to just deal with the conflict rather than spend thirty minutes assessing blame. In any given conflict, the scales tip one way or the other, but our job cannot be fault-finder. Our job has to be peacemaker.

In today's world, many of us, including me, face the dilemma of blending two families into one. According to Pew Research Center, 16 percent of children live in a blended family. That's a lot of children waking up each day to face relationship obstacles they didn't create. Dealing with biological siblings is hard enough. Now consider what it takes to blend new siblings who have possibly been raised with a different set of rules and behaviors. As a grandparent, it's our responsibility to ease our grands' burdens and to be helpers—exactly what Paul was asking his friends to be. In the NIV translation, Paul says to Euodia and Syntyche's friends, "I ask you, my true companion, *help* these women since they have contended at my side in the cause of the gospel, along with Clement and the rest of my co-workers, whose names are in the book of life" (Philippians 4:3, emphasis mine). He doesn't say, "Choose a side," or even, "Stay out of it." He simply says, "Help these women."

After my son's divorce, I will never forget how my sweet granddaughter asked, "Will you help us?" That was a powerful moment. I had to decide what *help* would look like. Of course I would help with the practical tasks such as getting the kids to school, overseeing homework, cooking, shopping for clothes, and on and on, but I also had to help with the intangible issues, including attitudes and behaviors that might come from hurt feelings. It was clear I could not choose a side. I needed to bring peace to a family in turmoil.

Grandparents can offer peace, and they can also be accepting and kind. All three actions help with blending and are especially needed when a new spouse is added to the family. Even if the new spouse doesn't bring children to the marriage, that person adds a different dynamic that requires careful blending. The word *baggage* always carries negative connotations, so let's call it "personal belongings" instead. Everyone brings his or her own personal belongings to the family he or she is joining. Those personal belongings include attitudes and behaviors that are different—not necessarily bad, but different. Granted, *different* generally appears to be *bad* at first because humans—especially children—have a hard time with change. But *different* really is just *different*, not bad.

So how can we help our grandchildren accept the differences? What's our role in all of this? I can only talk about my situation and hope that some of what we did might help you if you're facing a similar situation. First of all, any marriage that ends is heartbreaking for everyone. As the grandmother, my heart hurt for my children and grandchildren, and there were many conversations and late-night tears shed. But after a while, life has to move on. How can grandparents help a newly blended family smooth out some of the rough edges?

We immediately accepted the new spouse and bonus children into the family as if they were our own. Of course, they're not your own, but it's important that you act like they are until bonds are formed and your feelings can more closely match your actions. Until then, let your actions be those of God. Will your own grands feel a little jealous that some of your attention is now going to another child? Maybe. But that's life. As the grandparent, you must always take the high road as an example of loving and accepting people, no matter what the story is behind that person. This presents occasions to teach, and that's what grandparents do best—we teach, mostly by example, but we teach. It's more important that every child who enters your life feels loved than for you to give your biological grands preference so they "feel better." So what does that look like? Well, everyone's birthday is celebrated, Christmas gifts are given, concerts and ball games are attended, vacations include everyone, and lots of hugs are passed around to every child in the family.

Basically, the best thing you can do to support the new blended family is to be kind to everyone. Being kind doesn't mean there has not been wrong done to you and your family; it only means you've made a choice to rise above the wrongs and treat the offending party with kindness. All the little eyes watching the adults will take cues on how to behave in such a way that God is glorified. One of my favorite verses in the Bible is Hebrews 12:14-15. In the NIV it reads, "Make every effort to live in peace with everyone and to be holy; without holiness no one will see the Lord. See to it that no one falls short of the grace of God and that no bitter root grows up to cause trouble and defile many." I love that challenge to "make every effort." Like I said earlier, blending relationships takes elbow grease, but it can be done. Just hop up on that counter and use those muscles!

Hugs,
Chrys

Reflect on It

THE MOST IMPORTANT SINGLE INGREDIENT
IN THE FORMULA OF SUCCESS IS KNOWING HOW
TO GET ALONG WITH PEOPLE.

THEODORE ROOSEVELT,
TWENTY-SIXTH PRESIDENT OF THE UNITED STATES

After reading this quote, do you think, *That's way easier to say than do*? You're not the only one. It's the "knowing how to get along with people" part that throws most people into a quandary. Anyone with more than one child understands the dilemma of knowing what to say and when to say it to the different personalities you are charged with influencing. After a few failed attempts, it might seem easier to never attempt than to try and fail again. But if we think in terms of seeing others as God sees them and not as we see them, getting along with others is easier.

I worked with teenagers for a long time in my adult life, and people often asked me how I related so well with teens. I told them my secret is being interested in them and their interests. Even now with my teen grandkids, I try to stay current with what they are involved in. Not current in a creepy way, like copying their clothing or using their language, but in a curious, caring way—by asking about them and letting them tell me what's going on in their lives.

When we talk about blending families from different backgrounds, the same is true. The bonus grands you are now blessed with want you to know them and care about them. Your interest in them tells them they are not an "extra" but a valuable part of the family. It will be understandable that your new bonus family might be standoffish at first, but time will take care of that. Theodore Roosevelt said that knowing how to get along with others is a key to success. We know success can come in many ways. A success in a blended family is when everyone involved knows you love them whether they were birthed into your family or chosen for that position.

Remember It

Pursue peace with all people, and the holiness without which no one will see the Lord. See to it that no one comes short of the grace of God; that no root of bitterness springing up causes trouble, and by it many become defiled.

HEBREWS 12:14-15, NASB

Rock It

If you've walked the journey of a blended family, today might be a good day to write a note to your bonus grands telling them how much you love them and how glad you are that they joined your family. We all know the power of words. Those words can be life-changing (and game-changing) for anyone.

Grandmother Durham's Soft Sugar Cookies

Grandmother Durham lived in a log cabin on Saline Lake, located in central Louisiana. She always had cookies in her cookie jar for visiting grandkids, nieces, and nephews. (The original baker suggested doubling the recipe if you have grandkids around or there wouldn't be any to store for later. If you do, you'll need a really big bowl!) Grandmother Durham was Chrys's Aunt Gladys.

INGREDIENTS:

4 cups all-purpose flour

1 teaspoon baking powder

1 teaspoon baking soda

¾ teaspoon salt

1 cup butter, softened, or ½ cup margarine and ½ cup shortening

1½ cups granulated sugar

2 teaspoons vanilla extract

2 eggs

¾ cup sour cream

DIRECTIONS:

Lightly grease a baking sheet. Preheat oven to 450°F. Mix flour, baking powder, baking soda, and salt together in a large bowl. In a separate bowl, cream butter or a combination of shortening and margarine until smooth. Add sugar gradually to butter mixture. Stir in vanilla, and then beat with eggs until fluffy. Add flour mixture, alternating with sour cream, mixing until smooth. Cover bowl and chill in the refrigerator 2 to 3 hours to firm the dough. Remove 1/3 of dough at a time and roll out on a lightly floured pastry cloth or silicone baking mat. Cut out cookies using a regular biscuit cutter, or shaped cutters if preferred. Place on a baking sheet and bake for 7 to 9 minutes. Cool and store in an airtight jar or container.

I was dramatically shaped by my grandmother and my aunts because they convinced me there was always a cookie available.

———— NEWT GINGRICH ————
AMERICAN POLITICIAN AND AUTHOR

7

Little Ones Understand More Than We Think

1 (Shellie) wet the washcloth with cold water, wrung it out, and wiped my granddaughter's forehead, praying all the while. A raging fever, throbbing headache, and sore throat—none of these were in our slumber party plans. The two of us had capped off a game-playing, movie-watching evening with a little pampering at our homemade spa and turned in for a long winter's nap. By midnight Carlisle was standing beside my bed, nudging me awake.

"Keggie, I don't feel so good."

It'd been hours now since I'd given her some medicine to try to bring her fever down, and it seemed to be climbing higher instead. I wanted to know just how high, but my digital thermometer was broken. (Note to self: Buy an old-fashioned thermometer.) All I knew was Carlisle's scary-hot skin was warming the cold rag as quickly as I could dip it and wring it, and I was now officially worried. These moments were frightening with my own kids. Reliving them with sick grands tends to take the anxiety up a level. Was it time to call and wake her parents? Dip, wring, soothe, pray, repeat.

When Carlisle's eyelids finally grew heavier, I stretched out beside her, lowered my voice to a whisper, and continued praying under my breath. I was dozing off myself with more prayer words on my lips when the thought first formed. The words didn't feel like mine, but they carried a holy, recognizable weight.

"I'm not an orphan. You're not indifferent."

The emotionally charged words startled me because they were in first person as if they had risen from my own heart, and yet I knew I hadn't consciously voiced them. The phrasing itself exposed the naked fear behind my earlier prayers. Ironically, as strange as the prayer was, I found it equally soothing. I understood God was offering me the way forward. He was reminding me that He was with us. I've walked with Him long enough to know what to do next. I began to own those words by confessing the truth of them to myself and offering them back to the Lord.

Carlisle's skin beneath my touch was as hot as it had been moments before, but peace began to stand guard over my heart as I repeated the comforting words, "I'm not an orphan. You're not indifferent." It would be hours still before Carlisle's fever broke, but fear and doubt lost their grip in God's Presence.

I was still processing that prayer the next morning and reveling in God's goodness. How kind it was of Him to quiet my heart even as Carlisle's fever raged. I wanted my granddaughter to know what had happened during the night, even though it seemed like a weighty chat for her age. We were snuggling on the couch when I waded into the discussion, trying to frame the conversation in an age-appropriate way.

"This may be too much for you to understand," I said to Carlisle. "But have you ever totally believed in God until something started happening that you wanted Him to stop? But when God didn't stop it right away, did you begin to doubt that He was listening, even though you didn't want to feel that way?"

To my complete surprise, Carlisle nodded her blonde head with enthusiastic agreement. "Yes'm! That happened to me last week when Weston was so sick."

Would you lean in here and look at God's great big heart with me? Carlisle had worried about her little brother recently the same way I had worried about her last night, *and our God knew it.*

I told Carlisle how God had reminded me that He was a good Father, even when I couldn't understand what was happening and why. She soaked up every word. Afterward, we found a Scripture to help us remember the lesson. Then we gathered some water paints and a couple of canvases, and together we created some artwork using the phrase God wants all of us to know: *We are not orphans. He is not indifferent.*

I couldn't explain the mysteries of God's timing to a child when I don't understand them myself. I couldn't tell her why the Word tells us to pray about all things at all times when those prayers aren't all answered in the ways we'd like for them to be.

I could and I did tell Carlisle we were created for another world where suffering of any kind will no longer touch us. I told her that we were created by a God who loves us so much and who cares so deeply about our pain that He was willing to share it, all to make a way for us to live with Him forever.

Here's one of the most beautiful parts of that memory for me. My words comforted sweet Carlisle, and I didn't need to have all the answers! I simply gave her the greatest truth any of us can give our grandchildren—Jesus, the One and Only. With the gospel truth, we can offer them a sure foundation on which to build their lives. We can point them toward the divine refuge they need in our increasingly unstable world.

Chrys and I often talk about how sad it is that everything is magnified in today's public sphere and troubling news is always breaking at record speeds. Clearly, there have been hard times in our nation's past and difficult times around the world as long as it's been spinning. The difference is that we now see and know the details of every sad and scary thing as it happens, when it happens, with images aplenty to underscore the misery of it all. As if that doesn't cause enough anxiety, we're also waylaid with opinions on why it happened and what will happen because it happened! Have mercy. That's a lot of pressure on us big people, but it's worse than that. We need to realize our beloved grandchildren are hearing and seeing all of this incoming information too, and they understand more than we might think.

You and I can contribute to the fear and anxiety that reaches them, or we can create a peaceful atmosphere that gives them hope for today and tomorrow. We can do that by intentionally filtering what they overhear. Please understand, I'm talking about much more than our devices and ever-wired worlds. I'm reminding us how critically important it is that we guard the words coming out of our mouths!

As easy as it is to fall into conversations with other adults and bemoan the state of our world, our culture, and our politics, it's this type of woebegone exchange that paints a hopeless and dark picture of the future. We can do better. We're called to do better!

For our grands' sakes, let's temper our speech, learn to reframe the news in a gospel light, and remember that little pitchers have big ears! That metaphoric expression found its way into our language because it likens the ears of our little ones to the curved handles of beverage pitchers. I like it because it helps me to remember that my words, be they life-giving or life-draining, are figuratively pouring into my loved ones' hearts! It's a good image to keep in our minds on behalf of our grands, and for that matter, everyone else in our circles of family and friends.

I'm not saying we can't ever talk about current events in our grands' presence. It does us no good to try to raise our kids in a bubble, as much as we may want to try. But we can and must be aware of the tone we're taking about current events and the atmosphere we're creating with our responses to it. If all we talk about is how bad things are now and how wonderful they used to be, we're contributing to the world's anxious drumbeat and missing God-given opportunities to communicate truth to our grands about their purposes in this life.

We don't want our grands to hear us talking of yesteryear in glowing terms and acting like today's world is circling the drain! We want our grands to know they're not accidentally alive at this time in history. Our country may not look like Mayberry, but our grandkids are purposed for this moment! God Himself set the boundaries of our time on earth and where we would live. We can find this eternal truth beautifully expressed in Acts 17:26: "And he made from one man every nation of mankind to live on all the face of the earth, having determined allotted periods and the boundaries of their dwelling place."

By choosing our words and filtering our speech, we can give our grandchildren a sense of peace instead of abandoning them to the world's steady drip of outrage and panic. It's both our privilege and our responsibility to teach our grands that they were born for this day and hour. We can help them understand that their lives weren't determined by some random, cosmic lottery. We can let them know that their lives have meaning, and when they live with meaning, they'll live with purpose.

Hugs,
Shellie

Reflect on It

WORDS ARE CONTAINERS. THEY CONTAIN FAITH,
OR FEAR, AND THEY PRODUCE AFTER THEIR KIND.

CHARLES CAPPS, AMERICAN PREACHER

Sometimes it can feel like everyone around us is a lit fuse and we're one wrong move from the next explosion. Our every word must be guarded, our every action weighed against the potential consequences. Careful, lest someone blows! It can cause us to walk around holding our breath without realizing it, and that's sad. Let's stop!

We aren't meant to live on this kind of high alert. It's not healthy, and it leaves us perpetually drained. Worse still, it doesn't create the atmosphere we long to establish in our homes. You and I must learn how to step out of the madness and find peace if we're going to offer our grandchildren the stability they need to thrive. The good news? We have access to just such peace. The Bible describes it as the peace that passes understanding, and that's true regardless of our circumstances. True peace comes from knowing God, and Jesus made a way for us to be reconciled to God at the Cross. This salvation is available to anyone who believes in Jesus. But be warned; deciding to follow Jesus today won't automatically fill our souls with peace tomorrow. We won't know the peace of Jesus because we made a commitment to Him in the past. Peace is a present-tense emotion that comes from an intimate, ongoing relationship with Jesus, the Prince of Peace. Let's seek Him today—and tomorrow.

Remember It

~~~~~~~~

I will not leave you as orphans; I will come to you.
JOHN 14:18

Rock It

~~~~~~~~

Initiate a conversation with your grandchild based on Acts 17:26 so he or she can begin processing the empowering truth that he or she is right here, right now, on purpose! Hold your grand's interest by making it brief and age-appropriate. The goal is to lay the groundwork for future discussions.

Mimi Carmen's Icebox Cookies

We have it on good authority that Mimi's husband likes Mimi to have these in the icebox "for the kids." We're not saying he has an ulterior motive, but someone may want to make sure the kids get their share. Mimi is Shellie's aunt, even though she's only a couple of years older than Shellie. Backstory: Shellie's grandmother had a surprise visit from the stork late in life. She gave birth to a baby boy six months after Shellie's mom delivered Shellie! That baby boy grew up and married Mimi.

INGREDIENTS:

1 cup shortening
½ cup granulated sugar
½ cup brown sugar, packed
2 eggs
2¾ cups all-purpose flour
½ teaspoon baking soda
1 teaspoon salt
2–3 teaspoons cinnamon
1 teaspoon vanilla extract
1 cup chopped pecans

DIRECTIONS:

Mix all ingredients and shape into 2 logs. Roll in wax paper and chill. Slice into 1/3" thick portions and bake at 400°F for 8 to 10 minutes.

> *Think what a better world it would be if we all—the whole world—had cookies and milk about three o'clock every afternoon and then lay down with our blankies for a nap.*
> *Or if all governments had as a basic policy to always put things back where they found them and to clean up their own mess.*
>
> ROBERT FULGHUM

（8）

Their Thoughts
Are Worth More
than a Penny

I (Shellie) imagine we've all heard teachings on how important it is to "think about what you're thinking about." If we've
spent any time at all in church, we've heard more than a few
sermons toward that end. I'm not here to knock those messages. On the contrary, I heartily endorse them! I'm thankful
we more mature believers have been taught that the enemy
likes to mess with our thoughts and how crucial it is for us
to stand guard against his devices. And yes, I've got a grin on
my face as I resist the urge to clarify that description. I'll let
each of us decide if the mature reference is speaking to our
chronological age or our spiritual maturity. Instead, I'll share
my reason for bringing up our thought lives.

My concern is that we may have learned to recognize Satan's attacks against us, but we're slow to realize how early the enemy starts launching similar darts toward our precious grandchildren. My goal is to wake us up to his plans, Grandma, so we can combat them on our loved ones' behalf. It's far too easy for patterns of thinking and faulty perceptions to become ingrained in our grandchildren's little minds, and once they're established, they can follow them the rest of their lives. Buried thoughts are potent because they don't stay buried. They influence decisions and become patterns of behavior. I'm reminded of a wise observation that's been attributed to far too many brilliant people over the years to be able to name the author with any certainty:

Watch your thoughts, they become words.
Watch your words, they become actions.
Watch your actions, they become habits.
Watch your habits, they become character.
Watch your character, it becomes your destiny.

There's so much truth in that progression that we could break down and learn from, but here's the takeaway for our discussion. The wisdom of those words needs to be applied long before our grandkids are old enough to process it for themselves. This is where game-changing grandmas come in.

We can play a valuable role in our grands' mental development. We can help them learn to think healthy thoughts that will lead to healthy lives by teaching them how to recognize what they're thinking about, resist the damaging cycles, and turn destructive thoughts in a more positive direction. No one decides to think. It's automatic. But learning to think *well* is a skill that must be acquired. We have to learn how to take control of our thinking, and we can.

This means our grands don't have to grow up at the mercy of what's going on between their ears. They don't have to be subject to vicious cycles of thinking that limit their potential. But if we *don't* teach them how to break such cycles, we leave them vulnerable to the wrong thoughts forming ruts in their minds. Our privilege is to poke a loving stick in that wheel by teaching them how to invite Jesus into their thoughts to heal and teach, to comfort and correct.

One way we can do this is by learning to listen for clues. Our grands reveal what's going on in their heads by what comes out of their mouths (just like the rest of us). This means the grandson who says "I'm horrible at math" is already beginning to sabotage himself in that subject. He's shutting down and hampering his own efforts to hone important and foundational math skills he'll need in the next level of his education by listening to a damaging narrative. Sadly, if he thinks he can't improve, he won't.

Here's another example. The child who slides into your backseat when you're running carpool and announces that she "doesn't have any friends" is a child who's already learning to harbor a poor self-image. Even worse, she's engaging in self-talk that will become self-fulfilling when she begins to withdraw into her own little bubble in public situations in a misguided effort to protect herself from even more disappointment. She needs confidence, but she won't get it by believing that no one wants to be her friend.

It hurts to hear our grandchildren express those types of sentiments, doesn't it, Grandma? I understand. We'd like to respond by wrapping them up in big old hugs, smothering them with love, and giving them milk and cookies. (Oh, surely, I'm not the only one who wants to do that!) Of course, it's okay to do all of those things. We need to be their loving grandmas, and there's nothing wrong with fresh-baked cookies. I think cookie dough is downright therapeutic! But our grands also need us to recognize these moments so we can offer them a healthier alternative to the negative thoughts Satan would like to establish in their brains.

One of the most powerful strategies we can use in these situations is to look for the lie in what we hear our grands saying so we can tackle it with God's truth. For instance, the child who is bemoaning his lack of math skills is saying that he can't improve. He thinks he is destined to be a poor math student, but that is far from the truth. We can open the Bible and show him what God's Word says about learning and knowledge. It's not necessary to be a Bible scholar to find the appropriate Scripture, either. If you're new to finding your way around God's Word, you can type a question in a search engine and find help at your fingertips. For example, I just entered "knowledge" and "Bible" in the search bar and discovered this truth: "An intelligent heart acquires knowledge, and the ear of the wise seeks knowledge" (Proverbs 18:15).

Using this verse, we can help our math-weary student replace the idea that he can't improve with the truth that using his ears is the key to learning! The student who listens closer learns more. We can brainstorm with our student and find ways to hone those math skills. Some ideas might be doing puzzles and playing games together that require basic math skills. It could be using simple math in daily activities the two of you enjoy, including baking those aforementioned cookies together and seeing how that cup of flour is made up of two halves. It's an established fact that seeing concepts demonstrated helps us to retain them. Your grands' teachers might have other suggestions that can help them improve. The point is to help the child reframe the problem he or she sees as hopeless into one that has a solution, even if it requires extra effort! Everything that's worthwhile demands work. That lesson in perseverance is a win all by itself, and it's one that will benefit your grandchildren in countless ways for the rest of their lives.

Let's take our second example and see how we can apply the truth of God's Word to the child who claims she can't make friends. The Bible says, "A man who has friends must himself be friendly, but there is a friend who sticks closer than a brother" (Proverbs 18:24, NKJV). Those words can open up a great discussion with our grands about their growing social interactions. We can do this by reminding them that they have to be a friend to have a friend. Then we could discuss what that might look like for them. Unpacking what it means to be a friend can help them understand that one of the first ways they can change situations is by changing how they're thinking about them. You can teach your grands that when they look away from their own needs and instead look for ways to help others, it always rebounds to them in the end! You can also underscore that truth by reminding your grands that other kids might be feeling just as lonely as they are. Can they try to befriend other children who are sitting alone at recess or lunch? They'll have a better experience in school, and in every other area of their lives, if they begin looking for someone to include instead of waiting to be included.

And let's not forget the all-important second half of that verse: "But there is a friend who sticks closer than a brother" (Proverbs 18:24, NKJV). Jesus is the friend who sticks closer than a brother! Let's teach them that Jesus is always near and that He is the best friend of all. Hopefully, you and I have learned how our thoughts can affect us for good or for bad. Let's use our experiences and teach our grands to invite Jesus, their best friend, into their thoughts early and often. Put this in language they can understand by asking them to try talking to Jesus when they're thinking about something that makes them sad, or mad, or glad. Encourage them to tell Jesus how they are feeling, and they will soon discover for themselves how near He is.

Here's a closing truth worthy of celebration. As attentive and caring as we might be, you and I won't always know what our grands are thinking about, experiencing, or feeling. Take heart, Grandma! God does! If we ask, He'll be faithful to show us how to support them and pray for them through all the seasons of their lives.

Hugs,
Shellie

Reflect on It

~~~~~~~~~

IT'S NOT THE EVENTS THAT SHAPE MY LIFE THAT DETERMINE HOW I FEEL AND ACT, BUT RATHER, IT'S THE WAY I INTERPRET AND EVALUATE MY LIFE EXPERIENCES.

TONY ROBBINS, AMERICAN AUTHOR

Life hurts. It hurts some of us more than others, but nobody escapes unscathed. While it's true that we aren't always able to choose what comes our way, it's also true that we can choose how much of it we store in our heads and how often we retreat there to visit with our wounds. And now I'm talking to us big people as well as to the littler ones. Multiplied heartache results from not heeding the words of 2 Corinthians 10:5: "We destroy arguments and every lofty opinion raised against the knowledge of God, and take every thought captive to obey Christ." Our thought lives are crucial to our mental, emotional, and physical health. I'm convinced that after our decision to follow Christ, nothing is more crucial to our having full and abundant lives on this earth than learning how to think.

We don't have to entertain every thought that comes to

us. Legitimate pain doesn't have to become lifelong hurt. The Holy Spirit is willing to help us learn how to think well if we'll partner with Him. Let's be aware of what comes from our mouths after we say, "The more I've thought about it . . ." Because whatever comes next is shaping our todays and creating our tomorrows—and it all begins in our thoughts!

Remember It

As [a man] thinks in his heart, so is he.

PROVERBS 23:7 (NKJV)

Rock It

Dr. Seuss wrote a wonderful children's book titled *Oh, the Thinks You Can Think!* Find a copy, and read it with your grandchild to underscore the positive side of thinking! Even older kids (like me) can enjoy it and be encouraged to think well.

Nanny Crawford's Pecan Cookies

This treat gets a head start with store-bought cake mix, but Nanny Crawford says they're still homemade because they're made in her home. We love that kind of wisdom. Nanny Crawford is Shellie's Aunt Marleta. You can find more of Aunt Marleta's unique wit in Shellie's humor books. She has become quite the fan favorite.

INGREDIENTS:

1 box yellow cake mix

2 eggs

½ cup vegetable oil

1 tablespoon almond extract

1 cup toasted pecan halves

DIRECTIONS:

Preheat oven to 300°F. Mix all ingredients together, and spoon dough by teaspoonfuls onto cookie sheets. Bake for 10 minutes or until cookies are golden brown.

> *Grandmothers can always be counted on to produce sweets, cookies, and candies that seem to taste nicer from her than from anyone else.*
> — ELIZABETH FAYE —

9

Teach Them to Stand

The older I (Chrys) get, the more I understand that I can't solve everything. I remember as a young mom trying to fix every problem. In fact, I often joked with friends after a long night of discussing some important topic, "We're well on our way to solving all the problems of the world."

In reality, some things cannot be solved. Some things cannot be corrected. Some things cannot be healed. Some things cannot be fixed.

When my oldest daughter had four little ones, I was in the habit of meeting her family outside of the church building to help get all of her littles into Sunday school. One Sunday she pulled up, and six-year-old John Luke immediately jumped out of the car and began to climb up on the roof. Being the good and attentive grandma that I was, I yelled, "John Luke, get off that car." He quickly looked back at me, not wanting to be disobedient, and said, "2-mama, you have to see this." Of course, I ran over to the car to see what warranted a six-year-old to climb on top of it. Indeed, it was quite the sight. It seemed a frog had made the journey from Calhoun, Louisiana, to church that Sunday morning. For that twenty-minute trip, the frog had held on for dear life. There were twists and turns and ups and downs, but the frog never let go. And in the end, it arrived safely at church. Wow! Does that ever describe life! Sometimes in life we find ourselves attached to a fast-moving car, and the only thing we can do is hang on.

I can remember one such day in 2000 when my husband was diagnosed with stage-four colon cancer. If you've walked through a terrible experience such as this, you can understand our feelings of "this is so surreal." In our case, the word *cancer* had never been used for anyone on either side of our families. We had been blessed for sure, but that fact made the diagnosis seem even more strange. *How could he have cancer? Cancer doesn't run in our family.* And colon cancer on top of that! He had done everything right. Six years earlier, his urologist had congratulated him on coming in early for screenings and said he would never have colon cancer because the early screening would show the doctors any potential threats. So "why" and "how" and "what" were the beginning words of the next several sentences to come out of our mouths as we listened to the doctor tell us what our next steps would be.

We had surely jumped on a moving car, and it was clear we had to hold on tight if we were going to make it.

The next several months were not easy. Johnny had to endure radiation and chemotherapy prior to surgery and then more chemo after the surgery. There were sleepless nights and tears shed. That was now more than twenty years ago. Johnny was healed of colon cancer and has not had any recurring cancer issues. Are there other issues? Yes. He had a colostomy that required a complete lifestyle change. Clothing choices have to be considered and rethought. Sometimes activities have to be altered. But he's healed, and that's the important thing.

We learned so much about ourselves during that time.

First of all, we learned there are things in life that cannot be fixed this side of heaven. While Johnny is healed of cancer, as I said, there are other things he deals with that will never be fixed. Life will never be exactly as it was before June 2000 when my husband was diagnosed.

Second, we learned that while there is only so much we can do in certain circumstances and the rest is up to God, there are things we *can* do and *must* do. We had to find a doctor, and Johnny had to follow the treatment plan. We're grateful that Johnny's doctors were gifted medical personnel who calmly and confidently directed his steps to healing. We knew God was in control of the outcome, but we also realized that God expects us to be wise and discerning. We had to claim that wisdom and discernment and trust that God would help us make right choices that would lead to Johnny's healing.

Third, we never forgot that God is the ultimate Healer.

And after we had done all we could do, we stood in God's power and depended on His strength.

If you're reading this, you're probably "grandma" age and have lived long enough to know that death, disease, and divorce—the "big three Ds" as I call them—are responsible for much grief in life. Chances are, all three will touch you at some point and in some way during your lifetime. Any one of them is capable of taking you on a ride you never intended to take, and each one requires you to hold on with all of your strength until the wheels stop turning.

Two of our children are divorced. Going through divorce with my children was the hardest thing I have done in my life. I think it was harder for me to deal with than Johnny's illness. With the cancer diagnosis, I could see what a happy ending would look like; with the divorce, I couldn't see a happy ending.

At first all I could see was despair and hopelessness. I worried about the grandkids. How would they get through this and understand this is not God's plan for their own marriages? How would my adult children ever find loving spouses to be with for life? What will I say the first time I see the "ex" at a ball game? What about the former in-law parents? Would we still be friends? It was uncharted territory for us. There is no road map for all the side effects of divorce. Every family, every relationship, and every divorce is different.

The divorces taught us lessons as a family, as a couple, as believers. We firmly planted ourselves in God's Word and His promises as we strained to see what the future held and how we were to live in this new normal.

By holding on to what we knew to be true in our lives, we slowly began to see that brighter future. We knew God loved us and our children and grandchildren. We knew our family loved one another, and we were not going to abandon each other. We knew our church family would be there to support us. We knew that, whether we were ready or not, life would go on. By holding on to what we knew to be true, slowly but surely, our new normal did become normal. Every day we did what we knew to do, and after we had done all we could do, we once again stood in God's power and depended on His strength.

Are you a roller-coaster rider? Do you love roller coasters or hate them? In my younger years, I loved them. I wasn't crazy about anything that would spin in circles, but I loved a good roller coaster that had twists and turns and ups and downs. The worst part for me was always that first climb, when the roller coaster inches up and up and up before the first fall. All the way up, I could feel my stomach jumping like it was a gnat around a fresh banana. Once we reached the top the screaming would begin, but I loved it. Here's the secret to my love for a roller coaster—there was never any doubt about where I was going and where I would end up. You see, I never climbed on a roller coaster without knowing it had an end. Anyone who rides a roller coaster is given the same information. The twists and turns and ups and downs are evident, yet we choose the ride anyway because we've seen the ending. Are there things we can do to make our ride safer, more comfortable? Yes. We sit up straight; we buckle the seatbelt; we pull the seatbelt tighter; we hide our sunglasses and wallets; we hold on to a friend. But after we've done all we can do, we have to sit still and wait for the safe landing that's promised on the other side.

Our life journey is more like a roller-coaster ride than the car trip that unfortunate frog had to endure. The frog had no idea what the ride looked like and certainly no idea where he would land. Our life journey, if we're believers, will always end in the arms of Jesus. He's our safe place. Knowing that fact is what helps us get back on the roller coaster of life again and again. Every time, no matter what, our ending is the same.

Our grandchildren haven't lived long enough to know this yet. They are at the beginning of life where disappointments are small but valuable teachers. The tougher days are coming and, after having watched you weather some rough storms, they will be able to do it as well. I love Facebook because I catch a glimpse of lives I wouldn't otherwise see. Recently, a young man posted about his grandfather who had passed away. His words were so precious as he credited his grandfather for teaching him how to be strong and face life's challenges with a deep dependence on God. Even when we don't think our grandchildren are watching, they are. They watch how we handle our own life issues and how we handle the ones they're going through. For the most part, they don't need us to do anything but stand with them and let them know we love them. As we stand with them, they gain strength from us to carry on.

Hugs,
Chrys

Reflect on It

CHARACTER CANNOT BE DEVELOPED IN EASE AND QUIET.
ONLY THROUGH EXPERIENCE OF TRIAL AND SUFFERING CAN
THE SOUL BE STRENGTHENED, VISION CLEARED, AMBITION
INSPIRED, AND SUCCESS ACHIEVED.

HELEN KELLER, AMERICAN AUTHOR
AND DISABILITY RIGHTS ADVOCATE

Helen Keller's story is one of perseverance, courage, determination, and every other word that means overcoming. This particular quote says exactly what the Bible says in Romans 5:3-4, that suffering produces perseverance and perseverance produces character. Yet who wants to suffer? No one. No one gets up in the morning saying, "Lord, let me suffer today." And certainly no one says, "Let my children suffer." Suffering ourselves is one thing, but watching our children or grandchildren suffer is another level of misery. Someone once said a mother is only as happy as her unhappiest child. There's much truth to that statement as it's hard to be joyful when you have a child who's miserable.

Keeping the words to this verse and Helen Keller's quote in our hearts and minds will help us as we face life's trials. We do want what's on the other side of suffering; we want perseverance and good character for us, our children, and our grandchildren. That means we have to accept the hard times as teachers of those things. Very few people have lost sight and hearing as an infant and gone through the trials

Helen Keller did. Very few people have experienced what the writer of Romans suffered. Stories such as the life of Helen Keller and the life of Paul help us endure hard times. Our life stories can do the same for our grandchildren.

Remember It

> God is our refuge and strength, a very present help
> in trouble. Therefore we will not fear though the
> earth gives way, though the mountains be moved
> into the heart of the sea.
>
> PSALM 46:1-2

Rock It

Standing strong often means standing still. Praying for your grandchildren is probably part of your daily time with God, but today, take another fifteen minutes to stand in prayer for one of your grandchildren who may need extra support.

Gma Barbie's Anise Drops

Gma Barbie is Chrys's aunt, Barbara Shackelford. Because of her German heritage, she submitted a cookie most of us aren't familiar with, but it will be fun to try!

INGREDIENTS:

3 eggs, room temperature, beaten

1 cup plus 1 tablespoon granulated sugar

1¾ cups King Arthur Unbleached All-Purpose Flour

½ teaspoon baking powder

½ teaspoon salt

2½ teaspoons anise seed (This spice has a licorice flavor.)

DIRECTIONS:

Preheat oven to 325°F. Using a stand mixer or hand mixer, beat the eggs until they're frothy, and then add the sugar gradually, beating all the while. Once the sugar has been added, continue to beat the mixture at medium-high speed for 5 minutes. Whisk together the flour, baking powder, and salt. Add the dry ingredients to the egg/sugar mixture, and beat at medium speed for 3 minutes. Stir in the anise seed. Drop by teaspoonfuls onto well-greased and well-floured or parchment-lined baking sheets. Bake the cookies for about 10 minutes.

> *Baking is how you start kids at cooking in the kitchen. It's fun whether you're baking bread or cookies. With baking, you have to be exact when it comes to ingredients.*
>
> — SANDRA LEE —

10

Little Things
Are Valuable

*W*atching other grandparents take their grands to Walt Disney World, sail off with them on a theme cruise, or embark on a road trip to the Grand Canyon together can be discouraging if our situations are different and our budgets more limited, but we'd all do well to push back on that sort of peer pressure and hold on to our perspectives.

It's normal to want to give our grands the best of everything, but none of us can, and everyone is better off when we resist the urge to try. Grandparents don't have to go into debt to build lifetime bonds with their grandkids. Little Johnny isn't destined to a life of dysfunction if he never gets to shake Mickey's hand.

Thankfully, lasting memories can be made on every day that ends with *y*. My grands and I have been known to travel the world in our imaginations, and most of our adventures are free, or close to it.

Just the other day, my grandson Weston and I (Shellie) were in my husband's farm office. The grands call him Pops. We were searching for a hammer to use in an afternoon project when we unearthed a prize that held an entirely different kind of potential in Weston's eyes. Plastic antlers! Pops uses them to train dogs to track deer. I had pushed them aside, but inspiration hit Weston and he grabbed them like they were buried treasure.

"We could prank someone with these, Keggie!" he said.

Why the six-year-old immediately jumped to the idea of a good prank can be traced to yours truly, and it can also illustrate my point. Mind you, I never set out to hand down this particular form of entertainment. It happened by osmosis, a process *Merriam-Webster* defines as the gradual or unconscious assimilation of ideas and knowledge. That description fits my people like a glove.

My grands have literally grown up hearing stories of my good friend Rhonda and me pranking each other. Rhonda's grandmother name is "G," just one letter. It's unique, but so is she! The two of us have a long history of one-upping the other. We never know if she's getting me back for something I pulled on her or if I'm getting her back for her latest gag. The truth is, we don't really care. We just enjoy the game.

It's actually G who holds the distinction of being the

first to bring one of our grandchildren into the mix. One evening I returned home from a long speaking and traveling weekend to discover someone had threaded a bedsheet on a rope and stretched it between two trees at the entrance to my driveway. The sheet bore an ominous message in large, spray-painted letters: "Serious times! Be Prepared! Big girl panties for sale!" If you aren't already cringing with me, wait for it. There's more.

Tacked on at random to the trees holding this questionable sale sign were numerous big-girl, quadruple-large panties in various colors. How charming. I recognized the work of my BFF immediately. Removing them was going to require a ladder and some time, and I needed to unpack and start supper, so I shook my head and parked. I felt sure the beloved husband would be eager to help with the dismantling when he got home. He was, but I can't begin to tell you how much our town enjoyed the presentation before he was able to take the undies down. My meal prep was interrupted by a constant soundtrack of car horns, and my cell phone quivered with texts and social-media notifications. G's prank was clearly a hit. To add insult to injury, I knew G had hosted a little get-together with my granddaughter and another friend's child while I was out of town. I feared she had roped my own grand into her madness. My suspicions were confirmed the following day when I pigeonholed my seven-year-old granddaughter at church.

"Emerson," I said, "did you know someone tacked up a sheet near my—"

That's as far as I got before Emerson came clean, enthusiastically saying, "Me, Keggie! It was me! I helped!"

I've been told that proud little apple fell very close to this tree. I don't dispute it. With that one prank, Emerson was hooked, as were her siblings and cousins once they heard the story. Now they all love being involved in some good, innocent mischief, which brings me back to those deer antlers.

It was easy enough for Weston to choose our first victim. G lives just around the corner. We drove over and I let him out in her driveway to hide behind a tree. Then I went inside Rhonda's house to tell her about the buck in her front yard! I may or may not have given her other pertinent information. As far as Weston knew, Rhonda was totally surprised to discover that the antlers on the other side of her oak tree belonged to a little, blond-headed boy instead of a monster buck! Weston enjoyed the gag so much we ended up finding a few more victims at our church before we hung up our antlers! (Charlotte, Pat, and Carole, thanks for playing along!)

Maybe you think these stories are cute, but you don't have a prankster bone in your body. That's okay, Grandma! You don't have to have a prank up your sleeve. There's a message here that goes beyond deer antlers and spray-painted bedsheets.

Here's what I've discovered that may help you. What my grands are responding to is not necessarily the prank itself; it's the continuity of the story that we're writing together, and all grandchildren and grandparents have the opportunity to pen their own unique history together.

What I've learned from experience is that our grands respond positively to the familiar and individual routines that are part of their relationships with us. They're nourished by the simple patterns of these everyday interactions. The things we "always do" are the things they'll always remember. The moments we create and re-create offer a predictable stability that grounds them.

My own paternal grandmother didn't drive. By the time I was on the scene, life had worn her out totally and she spent most of her days in a green vinyl recliner in the corner of her small living room. Grandma Rushing was a widow who knew what it was like to raise a passel of children alongside her farming husband during the Great Depression. Life was easier for her by the time we grands came along, but those years of living hand to mouth had forever marked her. She could make a dollar squeak! It wouldn't have crossed Grandma's mind to spend money taking her grandchildren to Walt Disney World; and she would've scoffed at the idea. And yet, she was a game-changing grandma in her own quiet, dependable way.

I loved getting off the school bus at Grandma's house to be spoiled by her—I mean, to spend time with her. I knew the adults worried about Grandma's sedentary lifestyle, but finding her sitting in that same, familiar spot wasn't a detriment; it was a sweet, steady comfort. Grandma was never too busy to listen to my little-girl stories, and I had plenty.

I credit Grandma Rushing with being the first person to encourage my love of words, to make me think I could be a writer. As tight as she was with a penny, one Christmas Grandma saved up enough money to buy me a typewriter so I could "get all those stories of [mine] down on paper."

Walt Disney World can't touch that memory.

On the other side of my family tree were my maternal grandparents, living on the frugal salary of a pastor's family. There were no trips with Papaw and Grandma Stone, but the summer vacations my siblings and our cousins spent at their house were more than enough to seal them in our individual and collective memories. Those days came with lots of love, along with predictable routines we grandkids cherished, including Grandma Stone's peanut-butter candy and Papaw buying each of us a honey bun and a carton of chocolate milk on the way to his fishing camp.

Visits with our grandparents were full of simple but reliable acts of love, as ever present as the gum Papaw was known to keep in his pocket. I can still see him taking out that wintergreen gum and dividing it into two pieces to have enough to put in all of our little hands. Many years later, wintergreen gum brings me memories of Papaw Stone. I suspect it always will.

Bottom line: If you can take that group of grands on a road trip, by all means, go for it! But please don't despair if you can't. Nothing can take the place of the little things children come to associate with their grandparents. The consistency of our devotion speaks louder than anything we can give them, and our love will ground them in a way our gifts never will.

Hugs,
Shellie

Reflect on It

A LITTLE FAITH WILL BRING YOUR SOUL TO HEAVEN;
A GREAT FAITH WILL BRING HEAVEN TO YOUR SOUL.

CHARLES SPURGEON, ENGLISH BAPTIST PREACHER

I enjoy reading the biographies of people, just like you and me, who not only left legacies for their families but also changed the world for the better because of their great faith. I find it inspiring to follow along as God's story unfolds through theirs.

Although the ways God works out His purposes in their lives are as individual as the believers He's working through, there's one consistent thread in their stories that's similar to the concept we've been discussing: None of them become giants of the faith overnight. Their lives of great faith are built incrementally, one small, obedient step at a time. Like the little but consistent acts of love that grow into legacies, little steps of faith also create something special for our families.

Great faith grows from the obedient and persistent steps of little faith, by listening to God in His Word and in prayer and obeying what we hear today and tomorrow. So let's ask God to help us uproot anything we've allowed in our lives that's preventing our faith from maturing. Our names may not end up in history books, but we will leave a path our grands can see and follow!

Remember It

He put another parable before them, saying, "The kingdom of heaven is like a grain of mustard seed that a man took and sowed in his field. It is the smallest of all seeds, but when it has grown it is larger than all the garden plants and becomes a tree, so that the birds of the air come and make nests in its branches.

MATTHEW 13:31-32

Rock It

Identify something in your life that you want to see changed, and take at least one small step toward making it happen.

Gigi's Cake-Mix Cookies

Gigi is Shellie's oldest sister, Cyndie. (Shellie loves adding that chronological information even though she and her sisters are stair steps because she's mischievous like that!) Gigi says cake-mix cookies invite you to get creative. Use chocolate cake mix with chocolate or peanut butter pieces. Try lemon or strawberry cake mix with white chocolate pieces. The sky's the limit!

INGREDIENTS:

2 boxes cake mix, any flavor of your choosing

1 cup vegetable oil

4 eggs

Your choice of chocolate pieces, white chocolate pieces, peanut butter chips, caramel pieces, etc.

DIRECTIONS:

Mix all ingredients well and drop by teaspoonfuls onto ungreased cookie sheets. Bake at 350°F for 8 minutes. I take mine out as soon as they lose their gloss because we like them soft!

*I finished eating my cookies
before I finished drinking my milk,
so clearly, I need more cookies.*

ANONYMOUS

11

In Our Weakness, Grandkids Grow Stronger

*I*t's no secret that grandmas have lived a few years. You might be thinking, *That's an understatement!* Yes, we're "mature" as some people say it, but we know that's just polite talk for "old." It's okay. We've earned our years, haven't we?

Living a few years means life has delivered many, many happy memories, but it also means sad days have been a part of our lives as well. You've lived long enough to know that "sticks and stones" are the least of our worries. Sickness, divorce, job loss, death, and even words are worse than sticks and stones.

When my (Chrys's) oldest grandson, John Luke, was eight years old, he and several of his cousins were spending the night. I was busy with five younger grands who all needed food and baths and bedtime stories. I realized as the night went on that I had no time for my eight-year-old, who was typically my little buddy. But he was older and didn't seem to need my attention as much as the others. Still, I felt guilty. As I tucked him into bed that night, I voiced this concern to him. He sweetly hugged me and told me it was okay.

Can we all say, "Exhausted"? I climbed into my bed whipped like a puppy who had fallen in the back pond. I was determined to rise early the next morning so I could take a shower while the kids were asleep.

The alarm went off and I rolled out of bed, grateful the house was still quiet. I reached in to turn on the shower. As I did, I noticed someone had written on the wall with a red soap crayon. Then I read these words, "I love you 2-mama. From John Luke." Be still my heart! I hated to tell 2-papa, who is the love of my life, but that morning, John Luke won the "best surprise of my life" moment. I'm sure there was more than the water from the shower covering my face that morning. Happy and grateful tears were flowing.

Grandmas, we are going to get tired. Yes, we are! We're not as young as we used to be, and bouncing up from working that puzzle with a three-year-old looks more like we're moving in "slow motion." (Cue the low growl of sound effects as you lift yourself up from the floor.)

That night as I went to bed and that morning as I crawled to the shower, I was tired! Still, there's no way I would have traded my tired bones for the legs of a sprinter if it meant missing the message my John Luke gave me that morning.

God has given us a treat in our older years. He knows we're tired. He understands our weariness. He created the arms that have a little more shake to them now and the legs that quiver just a little as you climb a flight of stairs. He created aging. We might question His judgment as we look in the mirror and see the crow's feet in the corners of our eyes, but we can't question that He did it. He did because He created all things.

Here's a scene I will never get tired of seeing. My mother is ninety years old. She's in great health and the strong matriarch of our family. But she struggles going up the stairs and into bleachers to watch her grands play basketball or baseball. First of all, I love that she still wants to see everything the grandkids do. I love her heart for watching and cheering them on. But I really love watching her grandsons, whether four or forty (she has all ages with the great-grands), take her arm and help her up the stairs. She's so independent that she doesn't ask for help, but the grandsons know to stand beside her in case she needs them.

You see, maybe God created *our* weakness for *their* strength. We know He created our weakness for His strength to multiply, but perhaps it's for our grandkids as well. When I think back to John Luke writing that note to me, I have to picture a little boy sneaking into my shower and writing quickly so he wouldn't get caught. I have to imagine his eight-year-old heart having an understanding of what would make me happy and filled with joy on a day when I was tired. When I think of those things, I get it. I realize that God, in His infinite wisdom, uses me to teach my grandkids how to be kind, how to put others' needs before their own, how to be patient, and how to slow down. The lessons go on and on. In my weaknesses, they are gaining strength.

I am very independent. It comes from my independent mom I spoke about earlier, but I've learned to put my independence aside as I let my grandsons take out my trash or my granddaughters load the dishwasher. Those are two small examples of teaching by allowing your grandchildren to step up and help others. I don't want my grandchildren to think of me as weak, but I do want them to have hearts that are always willing to help others when they see a need.

I was a young grandma. As a young grandma, I jumped up from the floor quickly and chased the kids all over the yard. My youngest grandchild is now seventeen with the oldest being twenty-six. My sister, who is a year older than I am, has grandchildren younger than my great-grandchildren. I love watching her carrying a toddler, holding hands with a six-year-old, and lugging a diaper bag. At nearly seventy, she has nine grands that range from newborn to eleven years old. The reality is, as her grands reach their teen years, she will need a little more help getting up the stairs or into a car than I've needed, but I have no doubt her seven grandsons and two granddaughters will happily help her. And in doing so, they will become better people.

One of my grandmothers lived with us while I was growing up. My younger sister shared a room with her, and all of us got to "drive Miss Daisy" (Grandma Shack) around town as my grandma never earned her driver's license. After I married and moved out, two other grandparents came to live with my family. My siblings (four still at home) had plenty of opportunities to help our grandparents. My grandfather, in his eighties by that time, spent his last ten years going from the bedroom to a chair in the family room. A grandchild often helped him walk from place to place and served him his meals. My grandmother suffered from Alzheimer's. It was heartbreaking to watch her health decline because she was an active and very present grandmother. My mother took care of three grandparents at one time without a complaint or a request for help. As I look back on that time, I'm sad that I didn't help more.

We all learned what it means to serve others by serving our grandparents. We learned what old age looks like, and we understand that our time will come. We learned compassion and patience as we watched my mom attend to my grandmother like a seasoned nurse. We learned that our next meal or telling my mom a story could wait because there was a greater need. I'm grateful for the life lessons my grandparents taught me when they were younger and active parts of my life, but I'm also grateful for the lessons I learned in their older years. I know that in their weakness, I was made stronger.

Hugs,
Chrys

Reflect on It

HOW FAR YOU GO IN LIFE DEPENDS ON YOUR BEING TENDER
WITH THE YOUNG, COMPASSIONATE WITH THE AGED,
SYMPATHETIC WITH THE STRIVING, AND TOLERANT OF THE
WEAK AND STRONG. BECAUSE SOMEDAY IN YOUR LIFE YOU
WILL HAVE BEEN ALL OF THESE.

GEORGE WASHINGTON CARVER,
AGRICULTURAL SCIENTIST AND INVENTOR

As each day ends and a new one begins, we are one step closer to being old. Someone once said that "old age is ten years older than you currently are." I'm beginning to see the truth in that statement. I used to think the midsixties was very old, but now that I'm there, I put it in the "spring chicken" category. Okay, maybe not spring chicken, but somewhere in the early summer at least.

I love this quote by George Washington Carver because I truly believe being tender, compassionate, sympathetic, and tolerant are key traits to being a happy and healthy adult, no matter your age. These are the traits I want my grandchildren to have. These are the traits I would want the whole world to have. How do people acquire these traits? No one grows in an area without a catalyst for the growth. Our grandchildren need us to be catalysts. I admit, I have a hard time with relinquishing my independence (I can see my husband nodding as I type this), but I understand the value of allowing others to help us.

The Bible is very clear about the necessity of community, and I do not think God designed it that way so we'd become needy, whiny, and dependent on others. On the contrary, I believe God designed community so that as we learn to live together, we will be filled with the fruit of the Spirit. Your grandchildren are still in training with you. Keep up the good work. Let them help you, knowing you're really helping them grow up to be compassionate and caring adults, ready to change the world for good.

Remember It

We who are strong have an obligation to bear with the failings of the weak, and not to please ourselves.

ROMANS 15:1

Rock It

Think of someone who might need a hug or a home-cooked meal. Is there someone in need you can help? As the song by Diana Ross says, "Reach out and touch somebody's hand. Make this world a better place, if you can."

Mamie's Grandmother Chocolate Chip Cookies

Mamie is Chrys's sister-in-law Mary Owen, but her grandma name is Mamie. This recipe comes from a cookbook compiled by their local church many years ago. Mary submitted it under the name Grandmother Chocolate Chip Cookies.

INGREDIENTS:

½ cup shortening

½ cup margarine (or butter), softened

½ cup granulated sugar

1 cup dark brown sugar, packed

2 eggs

1 teaspoon vanilla extract

2¼ cups flour

1 teaspoon baking soda

1 teaspoon salt

2 cups semisweet chocolate chips

DIRECTIONS:

Preheat oven to 375°F. Cream shortening, margarine, and the sugars. Add in eggs and vanilla. Add flour, baking soda, and salt. Stir in chocolate chips. Form 1-inch balls of dough and place on ungreased cookie sheets. Bake for 10 minutes.

> *All you need is love. But a little chocolate now and then doesn't hurt.*
>
> CHARLES M. SCHULZ
> CARTOONIST WHO CREATED *Peanuts*

12

Lead Them to Jesus
by Going First

*C*hrys and I launched a lifestyle website called Rocking It Grand: Resources That Rock for Parents and Grandparents (https://www.rockingitgrand.com). It came from our mutual desire to help grandparents nourish the faith of their grandchildren. Honestly, there was scant opportunity for the "best laid plans" to go awry because we didn't have many. We simply knew we wanted to help other grandparents realize how tremendously important their roles were in God's plan.

The day of the launch we gathered a group of rocking grandmothers from among our mutual circle of family and friends, and when the big moment came, we used Facebook Live to announce this new community. Did it go off without a tech hitch? You're joking, right? We persevered, however, and a rocky start became a wonderful evening.

Oh, the fun we had! First, we introduced ourselves by our grandmother names. It had the markings of a traditional support group, minus the trauma. One by one we gave our most important bios to date.

"Hello, my name is Keggie, and I'm the grandmother of six."

Then we did what no one ever tires of in this circle. We told grand story after grand story.

If we haven't met you in person, please know we'd love to correct that. Chrys and I harbor more crazy dreams, including replicating that grandmother gathering all over the country. Wouldn't that be great? In the meantime, I feel a bond with you simply because you're reading this book. It tells me so much about you and the grandmother you want to be. I imagine one of your deepest desires is to be that grandma who models a strong faith for her grandchildren to emulate. Am I right?

It's a worthy goal, and one with the potential to intimidate us. We wonder how we can help lead our grands to Jesus without pushing them away. We're concerned about coming across as too demanding, which can cause us to err to the other extreme. So out of a sincere desire not to alienate our grands by pushing too hard, we can find ourselves holding back and *hoping* they'll follow Christ . . . eventually. *Hoping* they'll discover a love for God's Word, *hoping* they'll develop a prayer life. Oh, grandmother friends, let's not! We wouldn't do this in any other area of their lives that matters, such as their education or their health. We would be right up front advocating for them. Yet nothing matters more than whether they'll follow Christ. Let's not leave the most crucial, eternity-determining decisions our grands will ever make to chance and hope for the best. We don't have to be intimidated by the responsibilities of this role. There's another way, a better way, and the Lord is ever ready to partner with us in it.

I have three suggestions that can help. You can implement them as reinforcements for their parents if they're raising your grands in the faith. Or you can be that person who lives like Jesus before your grands in a way they aren't seeing at home. Either way, do consider what I call the "ABCs of Leading Your Grands to Jesus."

Always Be Growing in Christ. Never settle for what you know of Jesus. It starts here because there's no leading from behind. If we're always yielding and drawing closer to Christ in our own lives, we can trust that His life in us will be drawing those around us. Everything about our lives can point inquisitive little minds to the God with all the answers!

My oldest grandson has always been very observant. I learned early on to recognize his pensive look, the adorable way he had of leaning his head to one side and scrunching up his forehead as if he were trying to decide the best way to proceed. It meant a question was coming, and it was going to be deeper than "Can I have a snack?"

Such was the case as Grant and his little brother sat at my breakfast table one morning. The memory is several years old, but it's easy for this grandma to remember the gaze of

Grant's beautiful, dark-brown eyes resting on a piece of wall decor in my kitchen that's embellished with one of my favorite Scriptures: "Whatever your hand finds to do, do it with your might" (Ecclesiastes 9:10).

I saw the wheels turning.

"Keggie," Grant finally said, "you have a lot of Jesus stuff on your walls."

I nodded my head in agreement. Grant's Pops (my husband) says a person starts reading on one end of this house and reads to the other. Grant and I grinned at each other as he waited for me to say more. "You want to know why, don't you?" Grant's affirmative nod led to a great theological discussion that morning on the most elementary level, which is precisely how I like to relate all things Jesus anyway.

I explained to Grant that because I love Jesus, I like to think about His words as much as possible, and I like to talk to Him all day long. I told Grant that a lot of times, I talk to Jesus even when I am speaking with other people. "For instance," I said, "sometimes, while you're telling me a story, I'm thanking Jesus for giving you such a sharp mind."

This puzzled Grant the Thinker. "But Keggie," my grandson protested, "can you hear what I'm saying if you're talking to Jesus?"

"Absolutely," I said. "Listening to Jesus helps me hear you even better."

That answer satisfied Grant, and frankly, I was relieved. I never feel like I can adequately explain to an adult the concept of holding Jesus in my thoughts, let alone a child. I'm always searching for better words to describe the joy I've found in doing daily life with Jesus instead of just saying my prayers and then relegating any further pursuit of God to the next devotional or worship service. One day, I hope to effectively expound on the glory of finding God in the marvelous mundane. In the meantime, I'll keep sharing His words with all who will listen. My words might lack clarity, but His are life to all who find them. "It is the Spirit who gives life; the flesh provides no benefit; the words that I have spoken to you are spirit, and are life" (John 6:63, NASB).

Grandmas, our once-upon-a-time-back-in-the-day commitment to Jesus won't move the hearts of our grands, but our present-tense relationship with Him will call to them! They can experience Christ through us before they ever come to Him themselves. If we want those around us to draw near to Christ, the most powerful thing we can do is draw ever nearer to Him.

Build an Atmosphere of Prayer. When we're with our grands, we can make prayer a natural part of the day. Of course, we pray with them at meals and at bedtime. But what about all the moments in between? They offer us opportunities to teach our grands about living with Jesus. If something good happens, we can teach them that every good gift comes from God and say, "Let's thank God for this!" If something is hard or sad, we can remind our grands that God will draw near to us if we draw near to Him, and we can stop and ask Him to help! I'm not suggesting we go into a long, drawn-out prayer over every little thing. I'm suggesting we demonstrate to them the joy, peace, hope, guidance, and ever-present help we find in God. It's not hard to model a life of prayer. We just have to be intentional about inviting Him into the day. "Rejoice always, pray without ceasing" (1 Thessalonians 5:16-17).

Heads up! This last tip may step on your toes. It does mine.

Communicate Your Own Accountability. Let's make sure our grands understand that we're accountable to God. That temper tantrum you threw in front of them, the one where you went beyond discipline and right on into a good old rant—even as you felt the Holy Spirit telling you to stand down? Yeah, that one. It may not have had anything to do with your grandkids, but they saw it. After you make it right with God in private, *own it before your grands*.

I remember years ago, I was following my young daughter through the house, making the same point, repeatedly. Basically, I was harassing her. God called me on it. I repented and then I apologized to Jessica. I told her it was my job to discipline her, but I was supposed to do it the right way. God had reminded me that He forgives me and lets me move on after correction, and I was meant to do the same with her. I explained this to Jessica in language a grade-school child could understand. Her eyes were huge. Mama was in trouble? Cool!

This principle can apply to grandmas who might not always behave perfectly. Oh, come now. I'm not the only one who's made mistakes. People see when we miss the mark, and those people include our grands. Don't waste the opportunity. Use it to teach them about repentance and forgiveness. "If we confess our sins, he is faithful and just to forgive us our sins and to cleanse us from all unrighteousness" (1 John 1:9).

There you go! The ABCs of Leading Your Grands to Jesus! *Always be growing in Christ, build an atmosphere of prayer,* and *communicate your own accountability.* Then watch as He draws your grands to Himself.

Hugs,
Shellie

Reflect on It

THE BEST WAY TO TEACH IS HOW YOU LIVE YOUR LIFE.

GINA GREENLEE, AUTHOR

I love this quote by Gina Greenlee because I do believe that the eyes of our kids and our grandkids are always watching us. They see who we go to for comfort and strength. Let's make sure we are pointing them to Jesus.

People whose lives display an intimacy with Christ can be great catalysts for our own growth. Can you picture someone who left an impression on your life or is even now inspiring you to keep growing spiritually? Maybe it's a former mentor; it could be someone you just met. Either way, take a few moments to jot down the traits that inspire you. Then ask the Lord to show you how you can grow in those traits. The best help is God's Word. You can do this even if you aren't a Bible scholar. For example, if you admire a person's calm spirit, you could search online using keywords *Scripture* and *calm* or *peace* and find a verse to memorize and meditate on.

Remember It

Nor do people light a lamp and put it under a basket, but on a stand, and it gives light to all in the house.

MATTHEW 5:15

Rock It

Grab a grandma girlfriend and ask her to join you in a new Bible study. You can find many free studies online. You could also challenge yourself to host a Bible study in your own home with a friend or two. There's no need to feel pressured to present the material like you have all the answers, either, so watch out for that trap! The goal is journeying together and stretching ourselves to do something that is out of the norm for us.

Great Nanny's Peanut Butter Cookies

Great Nanny is Shellie's mother, Charlotte Rushing. She's also known as The Queen of Us All. It's an affectionate name Shellie gave her years ago, and it stuck! Great Nanny warns us that this is a stiff dough. You may have to finish mixing it with your hands, but it's worth the effort.

INGREDIENTS:

1 pound butter
2 cups granulated sugar
2 cups brown sugar, packed
2 cups peanut butter
6 eggs
1 teaspoon vanilla extract
4 cups all-purpose flour
¾ tablespoon baking soda

DIRECTIONS:

Cream together first six ingredients. Add in the remaining two ingredients. Once dough is well mixed, scoop it out by teaspoons, and then roll and shape into balls. Place on greased cookie sheets. Take a fork and mash down horizontally and vertically, leaving a crisscross pattern on your cookies. Bake at 300°F for 10 minutes. This makes a big batch of cookies!

There's nothing more reassuring to kids than a plate of their favorite chocolate chip, oatmeal, or peanut butter cookies.

LAUREN CHATTMAN
COOKBOOK AUTHOR AND FORMER PROFESSIONAL PASTRY CHEF

13

The Puzzle's Corners
Keep It Together

My (Chrys's) grandpa was a good man. He was a quiet man, but a good one. Born in 1896, he served in the army during World War I and was a young man with a family to support during the horrific years known as the Great Depression. Like many of that generation, he was stoic in his approach to life. I've been told that his generation did what was laid before them, no questions asked. I'm sure that trait served them well, as times were generally tough and questions asked often didn't have answers.

As an example of his quiet spirit, we always knew his name to be Flem Matthew, but just before his death at the age of ninety-two, he told my mom his name was really Flem

Madison. When he joined the army, the recruiter mistakenly thought he said Matthew, so that became his name. He never questioned or corrected anyone who called him Flem Matthew.

I was born in Oceanside, California, because my dad was in the Marine Corps, stationed at Camp Pendleton. By the time of my birth, World War II was over, but our country was involved in the Korean War. Daddy was deployed soon after I was born and didn't see me again until I was a year old. That's one of the hazards of war.

After his deployment, my mom moved herself and her two babies in with my grandparents who lived in San Diego. They had moved there in 1944 to find employment during World War II. Jobs in San Diego were nearly a guarantee since it was a site of multiple military bases.

Only now can I imagine how elated my grandparents must have been to have us live with them. Having two little girls brighten their days would be a delight for any grandparents, and mine were no exception.

Grandpa loved to garden. He grew up in Atlanta, Louisiana, on 350 acres of farmland. I imagine the tiny yard he acquired in San Diego was shocking at first, but like everything else during war times, he made do. The yard was so small that one cartwheel with my skinny long legs nearly put me to the other side, but oh, it was glorious.

Grandpa had planted every flower and tree that his small yard could hold. As a child, I loved to walk into the yard and soak in its smorgasbord of colors and fragrances. It truly smelled as pretty as it looked.

Time marched on, and my daddy was discharged from the military. We moved to Stillwater, Oklahoma, where Daddy enrolled in college through the GI Bill. Being close to retirement age, it was best that my grandparents stayed in California a few more years. But they were not happy about it. I often heard the story of my grandpa being so distraught by our move that he developed shingles. (My mom actually took us back to California for a few weeks so he could see us. Bless him.)

Naturally, money was tight. Still, we managed a trip nearly every year to see them. Grandpa's yard of flowers always welcomed us back, as did the beach, Knott's Berry Farm, and the San Diego Zoo. All of that was fun, but we missed our grandparents terribly. Eventually, they retired and returned to their home state of Louisiana. As luck or fate or, we believe, God would have it, we did too. My dad got a job one hour away from my grandparents in Louisiana. Again, only now can I imagine the joy that phone call must have produced as my mother gave them the news that she was bringing five grandkids to Louisiana.

Grandpa's yard in Louisiana quickly duplicated the one in California. It was filled with plants, flowers, and trees that would grow in the Louisiana soil. It wasn't 350 acres, but it was bigger than their previous yard, and Grandpa took full advantage of it. Along the back of his property line, he planted a hedge of sugar cane. He knew about sugar cane since it grew on his parents' farm and provided income for the family of twelve. But in Grandpa's yard, sugar cane was just for fun. His grandkids cut it down, peeled it back, and enjoyed the sweet taste. Grandpa often sat on his back porch in Louisiana shucking corn or snapping beans while watching us run and play and chew on sugar cane.

As Grandpa grew older, gardening became difficult, so he turned to another favorite activity—puzzles. I remember sitting beside him for my first puzzle lesson. I was overwhelmed at all the pieces scattered across the little card table that had at least one wobbly leg. It was staggering to think how all those pieces could fit together and look like the picture on the box. It seemed like an impossible task, and I stated as much. But Grandpa calmly explained, "For now, just look for the corner pieces. That's where we'll start. There are only four of them." To anyone who survived a world war and the Great Depression, the word *impossible* should not be tolerated to describe the task of putting together a puzzle, but Grandpa never made me feel bad or ignorant for using it. He just kept his eyes on the puzzle. We quickly found the four corner pieces. Then Grandpa said, "Now look for the straight edges. They are easier to spot and will be the border that holds the puzzle together." Sure enough, soon the corners were in place, then the sides, and eventually, the puzzle did look like the front of that puzzle box!

I've often thought of Grandpa and the lesson he taught me about corners, straight edges, and borders. And as I look back, I can see the lesson applied to more than just puzzles. I see the borders Grandpa built in every home he lived in.

These borders provided structure for his family and joy in times of war and peace. Whether he meant to or not, Grandpa gave his family a space in which to thrive that was clearly defined and equally beautiful.

Whether they lived close to us or thousands of miles away, my grandparents were the corners and edges of our family. They held us together in good times and in bad just by being who they were and what they stood for. I haven't said much about my grandmother, but she's the one who prayed for us, took us to church, and modeled what Bible study looked like as she read from her Bible every day. Borders and boundaries—that's what grandparents are. We are the hedge of sugar cane, the row of glorious flowers, and the straight edges of a puzzle. We are the borders that hold the puzzle called "family" together.

Hugs,
Chrys

Reflect on It

IF YOUR BOUNDARY TRAINING CONSISTS ONLY OF WORDS, YOU ARE WASTING YOUR BREATH. BUT IF YOU "DO" BOUNDARIES WITH YOUR KIDS, THEY INTERNALIZE THE EXPERIENCES, REMEMBER THEM, DIGEST THEM, AND MAKE THEM PART OF HOW THEY SEE REALITY.

DR. HENRY CLOUD,
LEADERSHIP EXPERT, CLINICAL PSYCHOLOGIST,
AND *NEW YORK TIMES* BESTSELLING AUTHOR

The word *boundary* can make you shudder if you feel like you're being locked in and kept from something you want to do. (Remember Eve, when the serpent told her if she ate the fruit from the tree in the midst of the Garden that she would not surely die but that her eyes would be opened to good and evil? God's boundary was to protect His creation.) But when boundaries are handled correctly and their value is taught appropriately, those inside the boundaries realize their purpose is for protection and well-being.

As a game-changing grandma, you are so valuable to your family. You and Grandpa are the dots that connect the past to the present for your grandchildren. Your stories give your grandchildren security in who they are and what they stand for. Your prayers will cover and protect them. Your house will be a place of comfort and security. Grandma and Grandpa, know that you're loved for who you are as the leaders of your family, constantly wrapping your grandchildren in your love.

Remember It

But the steadfast love of the LORD is from everlasting to everlasting on those who fear him, and his righteousness to children's children.

PSALM 103:17

Rock It

If you haven't done a puzzle with your grands lately, today might be the day. Choose an age-appropriate puzzle, and use the time to talk about boundaries and the importance of them. Then just sit back and enjoy the time together.

Mamaw Lou's Easy Chess Bar

Mamaw Lou has three grandchildren and nine great-grands who adore her. She often brings this treat or a chocolate pie to family functions. She is the mother-in-law of Chrys's sister Joneal.

INGREDIENTS:

  ½ cup butter (1 stick), melted
  3 eggs
  1 box yellow cake mix
  8 ounces cream cheese, softened
  1 1-pound box confectioners' sugar

DIRECTIONS:

Preheat oven to 350°F and spray a 9" x 13" pan with cooking spray. Melt 1 stick of butter. Add 1 egg and box of yellow cake mix to the butter and mix with electric hand mixer. Pat the mixture firmly in the bottom of the 9" x 13" pan, covering completely. In a mixing bowl, beat the softened cream cheese and confectioners' sugar until smooth, then add 2 eggs and beat until smooth. Pour over the batter mixture in the pan. Bake for 40 to 50 minutes. Let cool, and cut into squares.

> *Opening the door upon arriving home from school to the heavenly aroma of freshly baked cookies leaves an indelible print in one's mind.*
>
> —— JEAN PARÉ ——
> CANADIAN CATERER AND COOKBOOK AUTHOR

14

Make the Best of Bad Situations

$\mathcal{H}$ave you ever considered hosting a camp for your grandchildren? Admittedly, it's not feasible for everyone, but if it's at all possible for you to gather the cousins together at your house for any length of time, Grandma, do it! You won't regret it. There are family bonds to be strengthened, lifetime memories to be made, and countless opportunities to strengthen your grands' faith and reaffirm the lessons their parents are instilling. And if their parents aren't giving them that sure foundation, well, you can start! (Bonus? Those frontline warriors known as their parents will appreciate your giving them a well-deserved break!)

I (Shellie) have been hosting a camp for our grands for

the last four summers, and it's always a toss-up as to who is the most excited when it rolls around. Frankly, it's a mighty close race between the grandchildren and Keggie here. Our gathering is officially called Pops and Keggie Kamp, but the grands habitually shorten our official moniker to Keggie Kamp, regardless of my efforts to include the beloved farmer. This can be equally attributed to the fact that Pops still has to farm during the lovely chaos of it all, and the reality that he functions more like the wise manager of this crowd as compared to Keggie, fellow Kamper. Our Kamp hashtag says it all: #noadultsallowed. We print it on our T-shirts and on our crafts, and none of the grands think it disqualifies me or my BFF, who is known to hang at the lake with us.

Our gathering is full of nonstop activity. Among the items to be checked off our ever-growing list are the requisite tube-till-you-drop afternoons on the lake, devotions with memory verses and crafts, visits with their great-grandparents who live down the road, and four-wheeler rides around the farm. Together we have loads of fun and consume large amounts of food that's not always heavy on the fruits and veggies! Afterward, I post a gazillion pictures of them on social media. Because I can.

That was the highlight reel. Now how about some grittier, behind-the-scenes action? As fun as Kamp is for all of us, it never fails to provide its fair share of folly, too. Lean in and I'll tell you a story about one of my ginormous grandparenting fails. That's right. Littles aren't the only ones who can fall into folly.

The grands and I were headed out on the lake for an afternoon of boating and swimming. That particular day I was the only big person in the party, so we weren't going to be tubing, skiing, or kneeboarding. (For water sports, we insist on having a grown-up at the wheel and grown-up eyes on those being towed.)

The grands and I had all trooped down to the boat dock, carrying the necessary supplies. The kids toted beach towels and extra sunscreen. I carried a cooler of ice-cold drinks and a big bag of snacks. Lake fun requires many snacks. We consider it fuel. Let the record show that up until the big grandma fail, I had been strenuously following all of our important safety rules. The kids were already covered in sunscreen and wearing their life vests, having suited up before we ever headed for the dock.

The kids were all seated, and I was pulling away from the dock when I noticed it. Bummer! We had inadvertently left the cooler on the lower level of the dock. I made a large circle and trolled back up to the dock, slowly. There was zero wind, and the boat was resting motionless in the water, which is when I made the big mistake I can't possibly defend. My serious lapse in judgment could have ended very badly. I've thanked Jesus a hundred thousand times that it didn't! But back to the story.

I instructed the grands to keep their seats. My intention was to step off the boat's back platform, grab the cooler, and step right back on the boat. Sounds fine, right? And it would have been, if only I had killed the motor.

In that precise nanosecond of time as I stepped off the boat, the middle grandchild decided to act. From what we could piece together later, Connor thought said vessel was going to drift away without me. So in typical-Connor, ninja-speed fashion, the seven-year-old said, "I'll help, Keggie!" The next second has been forever recorded in my memory, in slow motion.

As Ninja Connor was announcing his plan to help, he simultaneously teleported himself to the gearshift and pulled it downward in one fluid motion. Before my eyes, my grands began leaving the dock, without me—in reverse!

Pandemonium ensued. Somehow, with all five grands screaming over my instructions, Connor's older brother had the presence of mind to remove the keys from the ignition, thus killing the motor. Thank you, nine-year-old grandson. Thank you very much for showing more maturity than your grandma. Unfortunately, the horror wasn't over. There sat my grands, in the boat all by themselves, quite a distance from the dock. I could hear the older grands trying to quiet their younger siblings as I searched for an option beyond the obvious. There was none. I was about to do what I didn't want to do and what I try my best never to do. Be still my fearful heart. I was about to swim off the dock.

I've made it my life's mission not to swim off of the same dock here in northeast Louisiana where I regularly see snakes sunning their slippery selves on cypress knees. I have no interest in entering the water in the vicinity of where I imagine hungry alligators to be lurking in the shadows. Oh, no, ma'am. I am your original summer bum. I love it. It's my favorite season. I tube, ski, kneeboard—all of it! I just do it from the center of the lake. Everyone knows this. My friends know this. My family knows this. My grands know this. This is what is known as a nonnegotiable. Keggie enters the water from the boat in the middle of the lake, and she returns to the boat in the middle of the lake, at least in normal times. These were not normal times.

There may be a pause here in action as I retell the story, but those were my grandchildren out there in that boat. So rest assured, there was no pause that day. I removed my sunglasses, phone, and swimsuit cover and dove in.

As I stroked through the water toward the boat, its occupants grew quiet. They'd all been fussing at Connor until I dove in, but that stopped when they watched Keggie breaking her nonnegotiable. Keggie was not going to be happy once she boarded, and they knew it.

Emerson Ann, the oldest granddaughter, moved toward the rear of the boat slowly as I drew near. "I'm just lowering the ladder for you, Keggie," she said, in the gentle, pacifying tone one might use to approach a growling dog. Mission accomplished, she quickly returned to her seat.

Not a word was said as I boarded. Five pairs of eyes watched me warily as I toweled off and endeavored to catch my breath. Everyone was waiting for the sermon that was sure to come. I could hear the sound of Connor's uneven breathing as he willed himself to quit crying. I looked up and met his beautiful, dark eyes, clouded with anxiety and still wet with tears, and I smiled. There would be ample time to talk about what went wrong. The moment called for more than that.

"Let's talk," I said to the grands as I pulled Connor into my arms. I fired up the motor, pulled to the middle of the lake, and turned it off. Then we grabbed the snacks and settled in for a chat. Those grands couldn't have listened any closer as we began talking about the choices we make and how they can have consequences far beyond what we may intend. I had their full attention as we talked about how God can help us learn to make better choices.

Among other things, I told Connor I knew he meant well when he disobeyed the order to sit still, but I reminded him that another of our rules was that they never touch the throttle, the wheel, or the keys. Connor was obviously contrite. The others had heard him crying and saying "I'm sorry!" more than once. We all knew he acted wrongly. I made sure Connor and the other kids understood he was also forgiven, and we weren't going to spend the rest of the day reminding him of his mistakes. I reminded the grands that when we ask the Lord to forgive us, He does. Then He forgets our sins and allows us to start again. He expects us to offer each other the same kind of do-overs.

I also told them that I'd made the first mistake by not turning off the boat motor. Grown-ups can make mistakes too, I said, and I'd made a big one. We said a prayer to thank God for His protection, wiped our eyes, and salvaged the day.

By the weekend, their parents had arrived and our larger family reunion began. We were all sitting around a dinner table strewn with empty dishes, telling stories on full stomachs, which happens to be one of my favorite things in all the world.

I'm sure I was going to tell the other adults about our mishap, eventually, when the time was right. Except . . . during a story-swapping conversation about near misses, Emerson blurted out, "Like when we drove the boat without you, Keggie?"

My granddaughter froze with an "Oh no, I'm sorry" look on her face, and every adult eye in the room swiveled to Keggie. *Ruh-roh.* Sometimes you don't get to choose your moment of reckoning.

In the end, all was well. The grands' parents were gracious about my mistake, and grace upon grace, they still trust me with their littles.

Teaching opportunities abound whenever we're with our grands, in the good times and bad, and yes, in the perilous situations too. Game-changing grandmas learn to make the best of bad situations. With heaven's help, we can redeem everyday moments and create lifetime memories by taking a deep breath and modeling the grace of God.

Hugs,
Shellie

Reflect on It

THINGS TURN OUT BEST FOR THE PEOPLE WHO MAKE
THE BEST OF THE WAY THINGS TURN OUT.

JOHN WOODEN, AMERICAN BASKETBALL COACH

My sisters and I thought our Papa had a strange way of responding to bad situations when we were little. I can remember him hitting his thumb with a hammer and exclaiming, "Thank You, Lord, for a thumb to get hurt." Papa also thought we should laugh when we hit our elbows, or as he called them, our "funny bones." Never you mind the pain radiating up and down our arms. I'm not sure if anyone even talks about funny bones anymore, but I understand the lesson my dad was teaching, and it applies to every generation.

One of the surest ways to learn how to make the best of bad situations is by cultivating a grateful heart, and that's something within everyone's reach. While it might be true that some people are more naturally positive than others, I believe expressing gratitude is a learned behavior. We've all seen the memes saying, "There's always something to be grateful for!" Let's ask God for eyes to see so we can pass on positive perspectives to our grands.

Remember It

Be filled with the Spirit, speaking to one another in psalms and hymns and spiritual songs, singing and making melody with your hearts to the Lord; always giving thanks for all things in the name of our Lord Jesus Christ to our God and Father.

EPHESIANS 5:18-20, NASB

Rock It

~~~~~~

Think of a hard situation you've gone through and identify something good that came out of it. Jot down a prayer of gratitude, and slip it into your Bible to remind yourself to look for the silver lining.

Nana Judy's Tea Cakes

Nana Judy is Shellie's mom's baby sister, Judy Patrick. Rumor has it Nana Judy has been known to bring her tea cakes to the hospital when the family has waiting-room duty for a loved one. Once there, she also passes them out to strangers who quickly become friends.

INGREDIENTS:

    1 cup (2 sticks) butter, softened
    1 cup granulated sugar
    1 teaspoon vanilla extract
    ½ teaspoon lemon extract
    1 egg
    ½ teaspoon baking soda
    ¼ teaspoon salt
    2½ cups all-purpose flour, sifted

DIRECTIONS:

Cream butter, sugar, vanilla, and lemon extract. Add egg, baking soda, and salt. Gradually stir in the flour. Once it's fully incorporated, refrigerate dough until chilled. Roll in 1-inch balls, then flatten with palm of hand or bottom of a glass jar. Sprinkle with a little granulated sugar. Bake at 350°F for 10 to 12 minutes.

> *Home is where the cookies are.*
> — UNKNOWN

15

Things That Matter
Take Hard Work

*O*ur newest mom-to-be was in labor. A new grandbaby was on the way! Phone calls and text messages notified the family, and each of us rushed around doing what we needed to do to get ready for a night at the hospital.

We use the word *labor* to describe the birth of a baby. It's not an easy word. Or a glamorous one. *Labor*. Think about it. The definition is "to work hard; make great effort." Even with modern medical advances, birthing is hard. When you had your babies, it might have been even more challenging. But still, labor is labor. Sometimes it's nearly a day's work. The momma works. The baby works. The doctors and nurses work. Even the daddy has a job.

Things that matter take hard work, don't they? All of the important things—raising responsible kids, building a healthy marriage, keeping our bodies fit and strong, being a worthy employee—it's all hard. Easy isn't anywhere in the definition of doing life the right way or the purposeful way. As the matriarch of the family, you know the work involved in raising children to adulthood. Supporting and loving your growing family continue to take work. But you also know the value of caring for family. Family is valuable, and that means you'll work hard to safeguard it. We don't expend a lot of time and energy on things that don't matter to us, right?

As I (Chrys) leave the house on Tuesdays, I know that every house in our neighborhood will have their trash on the curb. No one guards it. No one looks out the window to be sure it's still there. No one cares. It's trash. But we guard valuable things. We take great care to lock them up or hide them so others won't take them from us. It takes effort to care for the things we value.

What matters to you now is probably different than what mattered when you were younger. And that's okay. It's as it should be. Priorities change as life choices change. As we watch our grandchildren grow, we might once again be reminded of our past priorities and values.

Our grandchildren, just as we did, will learn the value of hard work in sports and school, but we know they'll face tougher challenges than not being chosen captain of the cheer squad or the playground's "king of the hill." And let's face it, people these days are not as strong as they used to be.

Giving up seems to be the norm. If a child doesn't want to finish a season of baseball, Mom and Dad tell him to quit. If a child confronts another child on the playground and isn't "playing nice," Mom or Dad might choose to avoid the playground. If the homework assignment is too hard, Mom or Dad calls the school to protest. The days of kids having to work through situations are nearly gone. Still, hard days and difficult times await everyone.

As you know, two of my children went through divorce. This is not something I ever imagined. Even now, nearly fifteen years later, it's hard for me to write about. My heart broke for those six grandchildren who had their lives uprooted and completely turned upside down. What's a grandparent to do? How much do I help? When do I step in? One was my son, one a daughter. Do I help the son more because he's a man and needs more help with the children? Dealing with this situation and figuring out my role were hard.

One of my favorite quotes is "facts don't care about your feelings." So I took an inventory of the facts during those very difficult days.

1. Our family loved God.
2. Our family had not changed.
3. Both sets of parents love their kids.
4. We will get through this.
5. Looking different doesn't mean looking bad or wrong.

Grandparents are in the unique position of being cheerleader and coach with few strings attached. Do you remember your parents telling you something when you were young and then saying, "That went in one ear and out the other"? It happens. When we hear something from someone over and over again, we tune out what we don't want to hear. But, Grandma, you're not in the house or around your grandchildren like their parents are. You're able to speak to them in a way their parents cannot. As our family experienced stressful times during the divorces, it would have been easy for me to step back and not get involved. And I did that on some level. But on another level I stepped it up.

I stepped back by not taking sides or talking to the children about either parent in a demeaning way. In fact, I deliberately spoke kindly about the parents and encouraged my grands to include both parents in activities they were involved in, even if one of the parents couldn't attend. For example, if one parent wasn't at a ball game, I encouraged the grandchild to call and let Mom or Dad know how the game went. I wanted my grandkids to feel loved and secure in who they were as children of God and in our family. I continually spoke that over them and about them.

I stepped it up by being even more in tune with what my children needed me to do to help with my grandchildren. I cooked for my son's family. I drove kids to lessons and sports and anywhere else they needed to go. I invited them for sleepovers to give parents a break. I made myself available without being intrusive.

Learning the best way to be a game-changing grandma throughout these divorces was hard work—but it was worth it.

I always encourage my grandchildren's work ethic, letting them know that hard work is required for big results. Constant reinforcement of this important character trait can be the boost they need to practice or study longer, choose more wisely, and go the extra mile. If you invest in your grandchildren as they work hard to do life, your grandchildren will look for you in the bleachers during their ball games, call you when the report card comes in, take a picture with you at the end of the championship, and love you to the moon and back for always standing behind them and cheering them on. In addition to that, you will have shown them how to endure life's toughest days.

Hugs,
Chrys

Reflect on It

NEVER LET HARD LESSONS HARDEN YOUR HEART; THE HARD LESSONS OF LIFE ARE MEANT TO MAKE YOU BETTER, NOT BITTER.

ROY T. BENNETT

Hard things are just hard! There's no other way around it. Grandparents have lived through many challenging situations, and it's important to gently share some of them with the grands. While you don't want to one-up your grandchildren on hard times, young people today value authenticity. Sharing the tough moments and seasons in your life and how you overcame them can be beneficial to your teen and young-adult grandchildren.

I pray that the difficult lessons in your life have not served to harden you but have made you better. That's a message you can pass along to your grandchildren as you encourage them to work hard and to see themselves through God's eyes. That championship baseball game will fade away, but the lessons learned from either a win or a loss will last forever. The lesson you offer can be as simple as these words: "I appreciate how hard you worked for this game tonight. God values hard work."

Once my athletic daughter said to me, "I wish God had given me a talent that didn't require so much work." I replied that I'm pretty sure God intends for us to work hard at any talent He gives us. Keep encouraging your grands to make an effort. It will definitely pay off.

Remember It

For the eyes of the LORD roam throughout the earth, so that He may strongly support those whose heart is completely His.

2 CHRONICLES 16:9, NASB

Rock It

Take some time this week to write about a hard time you lived through and how you endured it. If your grands are old enough to understand it, share it now. If not, keep it for another time. They'll love reading it when the time is right.

Grandma Carol's Pecan Dainties

Grandma Carol is Chrys's Aunt Carol. She spent her life as a schoolteacher but is now a grandmother to two little girls. Aunt Carol most often brings one of her yummy salads to the family gatherings, but this is an amazing cookie recipe. Simple, but yummy!

INGREDIENTS:

1 package (17.5 ounces) sugar cookie mix (3 cups)
2/3 cup softened butter
1/2 teaspoon vanilla extract
1 cup finely chopped pecans
Confectioners' sugar for dusting

DIRECTIONS:

Do not follow directions on package! Preheat oven to 375°F. Combine cookie mix, butter, vanilla, and pecans. Mix well. Drop by rounded teaspoonfuls onto ungreased cookie sheets. Bake for 8 to 10 minutes. Cookies should be set but not browned. Cool cookies slightly, and then transfer to wire rack. Dust tops generously with confectioners' sugar. Makes about four dozen cookies.

> *Cookies are known around the world as biscuits, keks, teacakes and biscotti, and everyone has a favorite.*
>
> — JEAN PARÉ —

16

Experience
Is Worth More
than Advice

After my children were off to college, I (Chrys) took up the game of tennis as a way to exercise, but I also wanted to get to know more people in my community. Like many moms out there, I was so busy raising kids that I found I had very few friendships in our community outside of my kids' school and our church. It's not a bad thing, it's just reality. So I thought tennis would be a good way to meet people.

As it turns out, tennis has offered more than I could have imagined. As life rolled on, more and more of my family members took to the sport, and now we have entire weekends of family tennis fun. Since I've played for more than twenty years, I bring some experience to the court and pass

along tips to my grands. When my grandchildren are playing with me, my experience makes up for my age—at least
for the time being. There's no doubt my winning days are
numbered!

But the hardest part of knowing the game of tennis is
watching a grandchild play a match for their school. You
see, tennis is the only sport where no one can coach from
the sidelines. If you watch a major tennis tournament on
TV, you'll notice the coach must sit quietly off to the side.
If anyone suspects him or her of coaching, even with hand
signals, then all kinds of trouble break loose. That is a no-no!
In high school tennis, at least in Louisiana, a coach can talk
to a player between games, but a parent, grandparent, friend,
or foe cannot utter a word to the player during a match.
That's a no-no-*no*!

How does this relate to experience being worth more than
advice? Well, let me share how tennis helped improve my
grandma skills.

I was watching my youngest grandson's tennis match
when I learned a valuable lesson. Aevin has become a good
tennis player, but he's still fairly new to the sport. He's really
a baseball and basketball player but loves tennis enough that
he plays for the school when he can.

This match was one of Aevin's first of the season. The
ball came across the net and Aevin went to return it. But
he ran up too quickly, and as we say in tennis, crowded the
ball, causing him to mishit the ball into the net. As the more
experienced player (and part-time grandma tennis coach),

I wanted to jump up and yell at him: *Step back, wait on the ball, be patient.* Oh, I had a lot of things in my head. But remember the rule: no coaching from the sidelines. On the next play, Aevin did the exact same thing! *What are you doing?* I wanted to yell. *Back up. You're in no-man's-land!* But did any of those words come out of my mouth? No! One more time the ball came across the net, but this time, Aevin made the correct adjustments. He stayed back and patiently returned the prettiest tennis shot in tennis history. (Okay, not really, but at that moment it was to me.)

So I learned a lesson watching Aevin. I learned that mistakes teach us how to live a better way—how to do "that thing" in a different way for an improved outcome. I learned that I don't always have to tell my grandkids how to do "that thing." Sometimes it's best to let them figure things out by themselves. Have I been guilty of telling them how to do something instead of letting them discover a solution? Yes, I have. It's human nature to want to "soften the blow" if we see it coming, especially if it involves our grandkids, but is it always best? No! Sometimes it's better to just sit back and let them solve the problem. Watching Aevin that day reinforced that principle for me. I literally saw him figure it out and come out successful.

This is a little bit of a soapbox for me since I have worked with youth for more than forty years. As a summer-camp director, schoolteacher, church-youth volunteer, mom, and grandma, I have witnessed some attitudes and character traits that can be detrimental to future generations if we don't get a handle on them. Here it is: Our young folks today are not mentally strong. (At least our American young folks; I can't speak about the world.) I'm not placing blame; I'm just stating a fact as I see it.

But if I were to place blame, I would say it's partly because of our nation having been blessed in the last seventy years or so. We're three generations away from a war or poverty that was so severe it required food rations and breadlines. That was my parents' generation, not mine, and I'm sixty-eight years old. I'm old and haven't lived through what my parents and grandparents lived through. My parents struggled financially when I was young, but I've always had running water and an indoor toilet. I've always had food on the table and a roof over my head. So have my children and grandchildren, and praise God that they have.

But as talk-show psychologist Dr. Phil says, no matter how flat the pancake, there's always two sides. The flip side of a good life is this: Lessons learned just by living a hard life are not learned. It wasn't a tough life when I was growing up, but we did have six kids sharing one bathroom. The lessons we learned just from that one fact are numerous. I don't think my parents actually had to say the words, "Don't linger in the bathroom because your five siblings want a turn!" I'm pretty sure we discovered that on our own.

In today's modern world, my grandchildren have their own bathrooms. What? Yes, and yours probably do too. Or perhaps they are roughing it and have to share a bathroom with one sibling. In any case, you get the picture. Things we learned from living life in "harder" times our grandchildren will not learn. So what can we do? How do we instill character traits that come from experiencing harder times without them having to *experience* hard times? How can we help them become mentally strong?

I realize we're grandparents, not parents. As parents, it was our job to instill good character traits in our children. With our grandchildren, it's more like our part-time job. But it's a hugely important part-time job. For instance, if you have a part-time nurse, you still want her to be an amazing nurse. Grandmas, we are still important links in the chains of building strong character traits in our grandchildren.

I've been a very involved grandmother. My son was a single dad for eight years. During that time, I helped his family nearly every day. At the beginning of his single-dad journey, his children were three, five, and seven. It was a busy time, and I was honored to be a part of it. But because it was a daily thing, I didn't have the luxury of spoiling grands like I might've if I'd seen the children only occasionally. Many times I had to put my "momma hat" on and more strictly enforce rules than perhaps I would have done in my "grandma hat."

Many of you are in the role of granny-nanny and help care for your grandchildren daily. If that's you, praise God you're able to do that. Others of you haven't been called to that role or perhaps you live too far from your grands to help out daily. It's all good. There's no room for grandma shaming in this world. Grandmas today do not fit any stereotype and are probably more diverse now than at any other time in history. But it's true that living closer or caring for grands daily will require more of your "momma" skills. And when I say *momma skills*, I mean those skills that require intentional parenting dedicated to raising children into young adults who are mentally strong, responsible, supportive, and productive members of society.

Of course, I've no doubt that all of you want your grandchildren to be responsible, supportive, and productive members of society who are mentally strong. So what can you do? Here are a few things I've learned to do with my grands that you can do as well.

1. *Let them make a mistake and learn from it.* If you see your grandchildren on a more regular basis, remember my lesson from the tennis match. It's hard to put these lessons into action, I know. It's harder than it was with our own kids, but it's so important. Raising a generation of strong adults requires that they learn to work through their mistakes.

2. *Teach grands the value of giving back.* My precious mother-in-law visited a nursing home for many years. Every Wednesday, Mamaw would bake cookies and then take a few grandkids along with her. Those visits taught Mamaw's grandchildren that life is more than playing outside with friends; it's about caring for others. I started taking my grands with me on a

mission trip every year. The first year I took my oldest grandchild, who was twelve at the time. The next year I brought along two more. Eventually, all of my grands except one joined me on a mission trip. This kind of trip is not easy. It's hot. It's tiring. It's not convenient. But it teaches lessons children need to learn. I told my grands that there's no whining in mission work. And they never whined. They loved these trips, and now as young adults, they face life's decisions with a backdrop that includes having served in the mission field.

3. *Share your experiences.* No one wants to bore their grandchildren with life stories, but life stories are instructive. For example, on occasion we share one fact about an ancestor before a meal together. My husband will often find an interesting fact and type it up for the kids to read, or he reads it out loud. It's short and sweet, but it helps our grandchildren understand who went before them. For one of our family reunions, I created a bingo game using interesting family history. It was great fun, and we all learned about our heritage.

While I believe experience is the best teacher, I don't believe we have to be the one to experience it in order to learn from it. Our grandchildren can learn from our experiences. So let's tell them. Even the child who doesn't appear to be paying attention is paying attention. When we tell our grandchildren about their history, we're reinforcing who they are and what they stand for and believe. All of this gives children a sense of purpose and security. Of course, they can't verbalize all of that, but it's true. When kids hear about who they are from those they love, they are more likely to develop a good sense of self-worth.

For many years, I disliked the "begats" chapters in the Bible. You know, those boring parts of the Old Testament that say so-and-so begat so-and-so, and so-and-so begat so-and-so, until you've completely lost track of who the first so-and-so was! But now I value those sections and realize how important, influential, and life changing each link in the chain of names is to future generations. One bad link in the chain can make or break future generations. Our influence is immense, not just for our grandkids but also for our grand-kids' grandkids! Yes, our stories and experiences are critical to shaping our grandkids' stories and their experiences. Let's make them great!

Hugs,
Chrys

Reflect on It

A MIND THAT IS STRETCHED BY A NEW EXPERIENCE CAN NEVER GO BACK TO ITS OLD DIMENSIONS.

OLIVER WENDELL HOLMES SR.,
AMERICAN PHYSICIAN, POET, AND HUMORIST

If you didn't let the Oliver Holmes quote soak in, read it again. New experiences stretch us because new things require us to think and react in ways we haven't done before. My first tennis lesson was a fiasco—seriously. I remember thinking surely I cannot play this badly! It would have been easy to quit and never experience that humiliation again. But I'd already experienced it. So what would I do with that experience? I could return to the court and improve, or I could walk away. I chose to take another lesson. For me, it was the right choice. I love tennis. Even in my horribleness (is that a word?), I love it. For someone else, the right choice might have been to end the lessons. And that wouldn't be wrong either. As the Holmes quote implies, an experience stretches us to make a decision one way or the other.

Every experience leads to another experience. The tennis player who decides to quit will probably be prompted to do something else. The experience of not enjoying tennis wasn't wasted, since it probably led to a more enjoyable activity. As we watch our grandkids tackle new projects, we can help them accept who they are by being their best cheerleaders. Then let the experience itself teach your grands a little more about who they are and what they will become. One of my granddaughters once asked me why I was always trying to push her out of her box. She smiled as she questioned me, so I realized she wasn't upset about it. She knew I was helping her become the best she could be by encouraging her to step outside of her comfort zone. Game-changing grandmas inspire grandchildren to grow and *experience* life.

Remember It

For this very reason, make every effort to add to
your faith goodness; and to goodness, knowledge;
and to knowledge, self-control; and to self-control,
perseverance; and to perseverance, godliness; and to
godliness, mutual affection; and to mutual affection,
love. For if you possess these qualities in increasing
measure, they will keep you from being ineffective
and unproductive in your knowledge of our Lord
Jesus Christ.

2 PETER 1:5-8, NIV

Rock It

It's hard to make a plan for letting your grandkids experience life because life happens every day! But here's an idea.
It might be true that your grandchildren can operate a cell
phone, but can they make their own breakfast? The next
time your grands visit, teach them to do something their
parents may not have time to teach. Show them how to pour
their own cereal, flip pancakes, cook oatmeal, or fry an egg
if they're older. In other words, whatever you're doing, let
them do it with you. That pancake might be a little messy,
but you're looking at the bigger picture.

Mim's Crunchy Oatmeal Cookies

Mim is Chrys's sister-in-law Kim Shackelford. She treats the entire extended family to large trays of homemade cookies and candy at every holiday gathering. She's Mim to her eight grandkids who love to visit for warm hugs and homemade cookies!

INGREDIENTS:

½ cup shortening, butter flavored
½ cup brown sugar
½ cup granulated sugar
1 egg
¼ teaspoon vanilla extract
1 cup sifted flour
¼ teaspoon baking soda
¼ teaspoon salt
1 cup oats
½ cup coconut
½ cup chopped pecans

DIRECTIONS:

Preheat oven to 350°F. Mix shortening, brown sugar, and granulated sugar together. Add the egg and vanilla to the mixture and blend together. Stir dry ingredients in another bowl (flour, baking soda, salt, and oats). Add dry ingredients to the mixture. Add coconut and pecans, and then give the mixture a final stir. Scoop by spoonful onto cookie sheets. Bake 10 minutes.

Note: This is a no-raisin recipe because the grandkids won't eat them!

> *I love watching keep-fit videos while munching chocolate chip cookies.*
>
> ———— DOLLY PARTON ————
> COUNTRY MUSIC SINGER/SONGWRITER, ACTRESS, AUTHOR,
> BUSINESSWOMAN, AND HUMANITARIAN

(17)

Living in the
Present Is a Gift

*I*t's been a few years, but I (Shellie) well remember my first bout of SAG. And no, I'm not referring to body parts, although I've seen my fair share of drooping over the years. Every morning I notice that yet another part of my body seems to be giving up the good fight against gravity to party with Smokey the Bear—"Stop, drop, and roll, y'all!" That's sag, but it's not the SAG I'm talking about here. I'm referring to a condition I like to call "Separation Anxiety Grandma." You won't find it in the medical journals because I identified it and named it myself. But if you haven't experienced SAG, it's coming. Brace yourselves; growth happens.

My first SAG moment happened one morning at church. I spotted my granddaughter Emerson as soon as I arrived. She was running around with a group of friends. Emerson was probably around eight or nine.

I'd been on the road, traveling and speaking, and I was missing all of my grands something fierce, which may explain why I did what I did, but I don't suppose it will excuse it. Although it had been a long time since Emerson was small enough to ride my hip, my grandma enthusiasm got the best of me. I literally grabbed her up in a big old bear hug, lifted her feet off the ground, and held her (although I didn't actually sit her on my hip). I began to second-guess the public liftoff even as I was squeezing her to pieces. I put Emerson down with one final smooch and headed to find her younger siblings. The youngest one was definitely still a hip child.

Emerson and I were chatting later that day when I brought up my earlier embrace. I asked if I'd embarrassed her by picking her up in front of her friends. She assured me that she hadn't been embarrassed. But the sweet little thing was grinning broadly as she said it, and she has been raised with impeccable manners. Translation: I wasn't totally convinced that she wasn't trying to spare my feelings. I told her I realized she was growing up, and I would understand if she didn't like me hugging and kissing on her in front of her friends. "You can tell me if we're there," I said.

"Okay," Emerson said. And then she added graciously, "But I think we have a little more time." Oh, yes, I did melt.

We did have some more time, but soon enough the clock expired on public displays of affection.

Such is life. These ever-changing seasons aren't surprising to grandmothers. We know all too well how quickly time marches on. After all, this happened with our kids. Who doesn't remember sending her baby off to school with tears in her eyes? That was hard enough, but in no time those first-graders broke our hearts yet again when they moved on to middle school, and the middle schoolers made us weep when they hit high school. Then came college, weddings, and baby news.

Clearly, we have experience here. And yet, somehow, seeing the grandchildren's wings unfurling and testing the wind can be every bit as painful, if not more so, to our adoring grandma souls as it was on the first go-around. All is not lost here, friends. There are concrete ways to not only leave the door open to our relationships with our grands but also strengthen those bonds for the years ahead! Let's look at them together.

1. *Heed their signals without drama.* Around the same time the clock was expiring on public displays of affection with Emerson Ann, I had a similar moment with our oldest grandson. I was in Houston visiting our daughter's family and loving the Grand Boys of Texas, as I affectionately refer to those grandsons, when ten-year-old Grant gently pulled his hand from mine as we neared the front door of his school. Gotcha. Message

given and received. I gave Grant a big smile and continued on as if nothing had happened.

If our goal is an expanding relationship with our maturing grands, it's important that we recognize the signs and adjust without making them feel guilty about their growing independence. It's hard enough for them to understand their new self-consciousness. They can't explain why they're suddenly uncomfortable holding our hands, and they'll appreciate the game-changing grandmas who don't ask them to try. *No drama, Grandma.* That should be our mantra.

2. *Support them by encouraging their personal boundaries.* It's critically important for our grandchildren to be bold and assertive when it comes to recognizing their right to create personal boundaries for themselves. Let's be careful not to undermine their instincts. Our goal is for them to be confident and assertive enough to protect themselves from those with harmful intentions, regardless of whether the danger comes from within their circles of family and friends or from without. Obviously, none of us wants them to fall prey to someone who could pressure them to lower their defenses out of a misguided respect for authority, so let's be clear and consistent with our message. We need to recognize the responsibility we have in encouraging their personal space by respecting the boundaries where they draw them! When we make

our grands feel guilty about not being affectionate enough, even toward their adoring grandparents, we invite nuance into their immature decision making. Nothing is worth the risk of our grands getting mixed signals in an area that should be black-and-white. There are plenty of ways to show our grands we love them that don't include public displays of affection.

Kids can also go through seasons in which they figure out what personal and private space mean. A while back, one of my granddaughters decided she wasn't a hugger! Carlisle was barely nine years old when I noticed that she was accepting my hug but not necessarily returning it, so I asked her about it. Carlisle announced with great confidence that she just didn't like hugging people anymore. She added that she wasn't hugging her other grandmother either. I wanted to make a big deal of it because I'm without question an affectionate, hugging type of person. I'll be honest; it was hard to hold back. But I challenged myself not to push it, and I continued interacting with Carlisle the way I did the other grands, sans all the hugging. I can't tell you what changed or why, but that season passed. These days, Carlisle is the most affectionate of all the grands. I believe she's a hugger today because she discovered she could set boundaries and the family would respect them. She's in charge of the hugging, so to speak, and not at the mercy of it. Moral? We'll stay in our grands' good graces by respecting their personal spaces.

3. *Draw encouragement from our own childhood experiences.* You and I didn't stop loving our grandparents when it became awkward to sit in their laps. Not wanting physical affection didn't have anything to do with how much we still loved them. Growing up doesn't mean our grands have to outgrow us, either.

Our grandchildren are looking toward the future with eager eyes. Their worlds are beginning to open up, and they're excited about what they may find on the road ahead. Let's look with them and not hold them back just because we've found a comfortable place to sit down and quit growing.

It's a privilege to experience life with our grands, offering them the valuable perspective that comes with age. Having more time with them is a win for everyone as long as we resist the idea that they're growing away from us and embrace the truth that we can keep growing together.

The Bible teaches us that we can ask God to help us number our days so we can have a heart of wisdom (Psalm 90:12). I believe one of the ways we do that is by actively looking for something in every season of life that we can embrace. By not clinging to the past, we give those around us the gift of being present!

Hugs,
Shellie

Reflect on It

CHANGE IS INEVITABLE IN LIFE. YOU CAN EITHER RESIST IT
AND POTENTIALLY GET RUN OVER BY IT, OR YOU CAN CHOOSE
TO COOPERATE WITH IT, ADAPT TO IT, AND LEARN HOW TO
BENEFIT FROM IT. WHEN YOU EMBRACE CHANGE YOU WILL
BEGIN TO SEE IT AS AN OPPORTUNITY FOR GROWTH.

JACK CANFIELD,
MOTIVATIONAL SPEAKER, ENTREPRENEUR, AND COAUTHOR
OF THE POPULAR CHICKEN SOUP FOR THE SOUL SERIES

It may not be fair, but older people have a reputation for being grumpy. It's like the terrible twos, only it's the sour-faced seniors. You know I'm right. So what's this about? Are mature people destined to become sullen, or do we have a choice? I believe that as with every other character trait you and I form, we have a choice. I have a theory. Humor me.

I believe people who don't embrace change are the ones who become grumpy grandmas and grandpas. I've been on a mission to learn this principle of embracing change ever since I was a young mother, feeling pains because my babies were becoming kids. Those early months with an infant in the house are so precious. I was missing it already. I realized, however, that having a baby to recapture those supersweet days was the wrong reason to add to the family! That baby would grow up, and I'd need another . . . and then that one would grow up, and I'd need yet another. Unless I planned to be the old woman who lived in the shoe, I had to find a new perspective. I began asking the Lord to help me enjoy the season I was in, and I've made this a prayer through the years.

So have I arrived? Am I a perennially upbeat, happy person who just loves to see sweet seasons pass? Surely you jest. I can be as nostalgic as the next grandma, but at least I'm on guard. That's progress. I ask the Lord to remind me when my attitude needs adjusting, and I can testify that He is faithful to answer. We can embrace our todays and look forward to our tomorrows when we're walking with the One who holds them all.

Remember It

And even when I am old and gray, God, do not
      abandon me,
Until I declare Your strength to this generation,
Your power to all who are to come.
For Your righteousness, God, reaches to the heavens,
You who have done great things;
God, who is like You?

PSALM 71:18-19, NASB

Rock It

Challenge yourself to list three things you enjoy about your life right now—not the days past or the days to come but this one. Keep this list in your smartphone or put it somewhere handy where you can see it tomorrow!

Nana Sandy's Beach Cookies

Some grandmas raise the bar for the rest of us when they bake cookies! We're looking at you, Nana Sandy! These cookies sport gummy sharks and are the perfect beach treat. Sandy is one of Shellie's sisters-in-law. Shellie has three sisters-in-law, and she's scored some great recipes from each of them.

COOKIE INGREDIENTS:

  3 cups all-purpose flour
  ½ teaspoon baking soda
  ½ teaspoon baking powder
  ¼ teaspoon salt
  ½ cup (1 stick) unsalted butter, softened
  1 cup granulated sugar
  2 eggs
  ¾ cup sour cream
  1 teaspoon vanilla extract

FROSTING INGREDIENTS:

  ½ cup (1 stick) unsalted butter, softened
  2 tablespoons vegetable shortening
  3 cups confectioners' sugar
  1 teaspoon vanilla extract
  2 to 3 tablespoons whole milk or heavy cream
  Blue food coloring
  Blue sprinkles and gummy sharks

DIRECTIONS:

Preheat oven to 425°F, and line two baking sheets with parchment paper. In a medium bowl, whisk flour, baking soda, baking powder, and salt. Set aside. In a mixer bowl, cream butter and sugar together until fluffy and light in color. Scrape down sides as needed. Beat in eggs, one at a time, before stirring in sour cream and vanilla extract. Gradually mix in the dry ingredients until they're incorporated. Divide dough in half, and wrap tightly in plastic wrap. Refrigerate or freeze until firm and chilled. Scoop into 2-inch balls. Transfer to cookie sheets, flatten gently, and bake for 6 to 8 minutes or until their bottoms are pale golden brown. Do not overbake. Cool cookies before frosting.

To prepare frosting, cream together butter, vegetable shortening, confectioners' sugar, and vanilla extract until soft and creamy. Gradually whisk in milk or heavy cream one tablespoon at a time until desired consistency is reached. Add blue food coloring to mimic water, and frost the cooled cookies. Add blue sprinkles and gummy sharks! Makes two dozen cookies. Both the dough and the frosting can be made ahead and frozen to make for short work! Tip: Nana Sandy says they're better if time is allowed for the frosting to set.

> *Today, me will live in the moment, unless it is unpleasant. In which case me will eat a cookie.*
>
> —————— COOKIE MONSTER ——————
> MUPPET CHARACTER ON *Sesame Street*

18

Superheroes Don't Always Wear Capes

*W*hen my (Chrys's) granddaughter Sadie was in the fifth grade, the school planned a superhero dress-up day. Sadie went as me! I was so incredibly honored that this little girl who loves Wonder Woman chose her grandmother as her superhero. So that begs the question: What is a superhero? If I was one, I needed to know the definition. So I went to Wikipedia. (I know it's not the most reliable source, but we're talking about superheroes!) Here's the definition:

A superhero is a stock character that possesses abilities beyond those of ordinary people, who typically uses his/her powers to help the world become a better place, or is dedicated to protecting the public and stopping evil.

Wow! I was happy it didn't say "able to leap tall buildings in a single bound" or "faster than a speeding bullet," because those are two things I can't do. As I read the definition, I was amazed that it also defined the grandma role. The only thing not consistent with a grandma in that definition is the phrase "stock character," because a stock character is a stereotypical, fictional person in a work of art. A grandma is definitely *not* fictional; she's real and influences future generations in profound ways. Let's break down the definition to more clearly define the "superhero" grandmas of today's world.

1. *Possesses abilities beyond those of ordinary people.* You might not believe this about yourself, but it's true. You have abilities few on earth have. Others may gain these abilities as they grow closer to grandma age, but they don't have them yet because they're acquired by experience and time. They're available to any grandma who chooses to tap into them. What are those special abilities? First of all, a grandma is strong and brave. You might not feel all that strong, but you are. It's an inner strength, a mental toughness that is born from living through difficult and uncomfortable times. Grandmas know the phrase "The sun will come up tomorrow" is true, because they've lived through days where it didn't seem possible for the sun to shine again, yet it did. In fact, the birth of a grandchild is proof of that! Life might seem pretty

grim, but a new baby can bring joy to hard times. Grandmas can say that phrase, and often do, because they know it's true.

While the superhuman strength of a grandma isn't measured the same as a superhero's, grandmas are, no doubt, women of strength and power. A grandma can stay awake later or get up earlier than anyone in the household if it benefits her grandkids. She can rock a colicky baby, chase a busy toddler, and cheer on a budding ballplayer. Her strength knows no boundaries because of the love she has for her grandchildren. She might seem tiny and frail at other times, but if something or someone threatens a grandchild, she becomes as brave as a bear. I have personally witnessed a tiny grandmother scoop up a grandchild to protect her from a stray dog or another child who threatens to bite.

That's not the end of her supernatural abilities. She has supersonic listening powers. She might wear a hearing aid, but Grandma will turn it up just to hear the voice of a grandchild. When Mom and Dad tire of the words coming out of their children's mouths, Grandma is there to take over. She can listen for hours. Questions that start with *why* and *how* are her specialty because a grandma is also extremely wise.

Yes, wisdom is her forte. Grandma doesn't care if her grandchild calls her at midnight with a question about a school project due the next day. She'll talk them through it with the patience of Job. In fact, my grands have done that. Since my background is in education, my grands have called me at all hours of the night and day for help with homework. No matter what I'd done that day, answering my grandchild's question was an extremely important task.

Another grandma superpower is patience. A grandma can sit on the porch for hours watching a grandchild turn cartwheels or throw a baseball. She can patiently teach a five-year-old how to tie his shoes and coach a fifteen-year-old through driving lessons.

From toddlers to teens, she never tires of being with her grandchildren, even if their behavior is considered rowdy. That's because she also possesses the superpower of unconditional love. Grandma never puts qualifiers on her love. Even if a grandkid's grades aren't what they should be or a grandchild wasn't nice in the grocery store, a grandma will still hold her arms wide open and give the biggest hug she can manage. A grandma's love for her grandchildren is one that is hard to explain and so important to the development of a child. A child needs to know that no matter what happens, Grandma's heart is always there for him or her. It's a stabilizer—one that can make a difference in children's lives as they make important choices for their future. A stable child makes better choices in life. Yes, a grandma is a super-hero because she possesses powers beyond ordinary people. She's no ordinary person. She's a grandma!

2. *Typically uses his/her powers to help the world become a better place.* Is this super-ability ever true of grandmas! Have you ever watched a football game and seen those

strong football players cry as they thank their grandmas for giving them the tools they needed to succeed
in life? It's a powerful moment of truth. A grandma
gives her all to her grandchildren. Not necessarily in
money, although Grandma is quick to pull out her
wallet when passing a gumball machine, but she gives
freely of her time, her hospitality, and her advice, all
with the purpose of making this world a better place.

A grandma's clock isn't the same as a normal human being's
clock. Grandma's clock always makes time for grandkids.
Giving her time to her grandchildren tells them they matter
to her, which tells them they matter to the world and challenges them to be the best they can be.

Everyone also knows that a grandma's house is always
open to a grandchild. Even if that grandma was a stick-
ler for tidiness as her own children were growing up, she's
now the opposite, as toys might be strewn from one end
of her house to the other in anticipation of a grandchild
coming over for a few minutes. Grandma's house always
has a cookie jar or a snack drawer just in case the little one
hasn't been fed properly by Mom and Dad, and hidden
away where Mom and Dad can't see it is that stash of lolli-
pops Grandma keeps in her purse to bribe for hugs and
kisses. Yes, a grandma's superpower of making her house the
"most fun" house on the block is a major covert operation
that begins when a new grandbaby enters the world. It gives
new meaning to hospitality as the house slowly but surely

turns into one big playground for any and all grandchildren to explore and use as needed for proper growth. Grandmas use their house to teach: to teach manners, to teach about Jesus, to teach cooking skills and how to clean. . . . You get the picture. (We know Mom and Dad have got this, but we just want to be sure!)

Let's talk about advice again. A grandma can give some advice, can't she? But she dishes it out according to her wisdom. She knows when to talk and when not to talk, because another grandma superpower is discernment. Years of living have taught her a thing or two about the appropriateness of words. A game-changing grandma knows that some words just need to stay in her head and some words can be powerful if spoken. It's a hard superpower to master, but she's spent years on this one. Sadly, she will admit, her own children didn't get the best of this superpower because it was still in the development stage. Now she has it mastered and uses it with confidence.

She's even able to use this power with children who are not her own grandchildren, which falls under the "make the world a better place" category too. She knows how to distract misbehaving children and set them on the right path by speaking clearly and consistently to them about what good behavior looks like in her home. Without question, the children respond with corrected behavior. Yep, that's part of how she helps the world become a better place. She uses her powers to help other children who are not her own. You see, once you're someone's grandma, you're everyone's grandma, so your powers can truly affect the whole world. I love that most of the little town I live in calls me by my grandma name, "2-mama." That's an honor to me—an honor that comes with responsibility. I take my grandma job seriously!

3. *Dedicated to protecting the public and stopping evil.* This last trait of a superhero (according to Wikipedia) might be the best trait of all—grandmas are protectors from evil and defenders of good. A loving grandma represents all that's good in any society. And a grandma holding an apple pie? All the better. She's the epitome of goodness.

One of my favorite things is listening to adults who give credit for their lives as believers in Jesus Christ to a grandmother who never gave up on them, who prayed without ceasing for their eyes to be opened and their lives to turn from evil to good.

My own grandchildren realize the strong presence of God in my life and my husband's life, and that has influenced them. Many times, one of them will call to tell me what happened at church that Sunday. I love that they do this, because it tells me they know what I value.

My mom is now a great-great-grandmother. She lives at the head of our street. We say she's the gatekeeper of our neighborhood. And she's perfect for that job because she's a grandma who loves and adores her family. Both symbolically and physically, she guards our street, which is full of family. Beyond that, she leads our family spiritually. She hosted a house church in her home every Sunday night until she was eighty-nine years old. She's the first to volunteer to feed a sick family member or a friend from church. She might be ninety years old, but she's dedicated to protecting us from the evil one. She often texts us, saying she's praying for one thing or another. She's no different from many grandmas who find themselves praying for their grandchildren daily.

Because many grandparents don't live close to their grandchildren, their presence is felt by the prayers they offer. I've been blessed to live close to some of my grands and hours away from others, but no distance can hinder the power of a praying grandma. When I can't be with my grands, a simple text that says I'm praying for them can make a difference in the way they face their day.

One surprising and glorious gift of being a grandma is the privilege of seeing life through the eyes of a child. Part of the "dedicated to protecting the public" role has to do with just being willing to be present in the life of a grandchild. Many times over the years, my grandchildren were in my house playing together, running through the kitchen while I cooked or peeking in my office while I worked. Looking back on those years, sometimes I wish I'd given them more of me. But then I hear them tell stories of being at my house, and I realize I'm in the story simply because of my presence. The fact that I was there, even in another room, was important to them. I provided a safe place for them to grow up, and they were watching how 2-papa and I lived our lives.

Grandma, you are a superhero! I hope you realize how special you are, how much of an impact you can make, and how God has entrusted you with superhuman powers to make the biggest difference possible in the lives of your grands.

Hugs,
Chrys

Reflect on It

~~~~~~~~~~~~

GRANDMOTHERS ARE VOICES OF THE PAST AND ROLE MODELS OF THE PRESENT. GRANDMOTHERS OPEN THE DOORS TO THE FUTURE.

HELEN KETCHUM, LOCAL TELEVISION PERSONALITY

Helen Ketchum has passed away, but for more than sixteen years she was the host of a public-access television show that examined senior-citizen life. The name of the show was *Transitions*. What a great title for a show about aging! But all of life is a transition, isn't it? We're not just transitioning into our senior years; we've been transitioning since the minute we were born. One stage of life follows another. That's why it's so important for us to be willing to model the behavior we want our grandkids to emulate. Even though we've included cookie recipes in this book, the truth is that being a superhero grandma doesn't even require baking the best cookies.

All it requires is loving your grandkids as if they are the greatest things since sliced bread. Your heroism comes from your intentional acts of kindness that communicate unconditional love and support to your grands. With just a word or a hug, you can be the game-changer.

Remember It

> Grandchildren are the crown of the aged, and the glory of children is their fathers.
>
> PROVERBS 17:6

Rock It

There are a lot of suggestions in this book. Take a few minutes to look back through the chapters and find some action items that appeal to you. Consider listing them in your phone's notepad or posting them on your fridge as daily reminders.

Mamaw Jo's "Grandma Cookies"

This is a constantly baked cookie in the family and has been handed down with a few tweaks from Chrys's Grandmother Durham. Mamaw Jo (Betty Jo Shackelford, Chrys's mom) makes this cookie now for the family, and they love it when she does! She's especially good at making a batch anytime someone is headed out for a long car trip.

INGREDIENTS:

1/2 cup (1 stick) butter, softened

1/2 cup shortening, butter flavored

11/2 cups dark brown sugar, packed

1/2 cup granulated sugar

2 eggs

1 teaspoon vanilla extract

3 cups all-purpose flour

1/2 teaspoon baking powder

1/2 teaspoon baking soda

1 teaspoon salt

1 cup (or more) chopped nuts

DIRECTIONS:

Preheat oven to 350°F. Cream butter, shortening, and sugars. Add eggs and vanilla to the mixture, incorporating well. Sift dry ingredients. Add to wet mixture, a little at a time. Mix in nuts. Roll into 2 log shapes, and wrap them in wax paper. Chill (I put mine in the freezer). Bake for 10 to 12 minutes. Less baking time makes softer cookies.

> *I think cookies are sort of the unsung sweet, you know? They're incredibly popular. But everybody thinks of cakes and pies and fancier desserts before they think cookies. A plate of cookies is a great way to end dinner and really nice to share at the holidays.*
>
> ———— BOBBY FLAY ————
> CELEBRITY CHEF, RESTAURATEUR,
> AND REALITY TELEVISION PERSONALITY

A final note from Chrys and Shellie

There's so much more to our grandmother stories we could tell you, but we know you're busy writing your own! Thank you for taking this journey with us. Our prayer is that we've been able to encourage you, motivate you, and help you truly understand the power and potential you have to be a game-changing grandma! We can all up our grandma game with faith, purpose, and vision. Let's do this thing! (Oh, and while you're at it, have a cookie on us!)

Hugs,
Chrys and Shellie

Acknowledgments

Our names are on the cover, but many people had a hand in bringing *Rocking It Grand* to our readers. Truth? That makes this part a little scary, but here we go.

Thank you, Larry Weeden and Focus on the Family, for the privilege of being welcomed into your publishing family. We don't take the honor lightly.

Thank you to Greg Johnson and John Howard for representing our work.

Thank you to Julie Holmquist for catching our boo-boos and shining up what we meant to say until it did!

Thank you, Stephanie Thornton, for lending your photography skills to the cover.

Special thanks to our families for allowing us to use the wealth of our shared stories to inspire other grandparents to seize this precious season with both hands and build strong foundations of faith for the next generation.

To our Jesus, thank You for everything. We owe You our all.

Index of Cookie Recipes

2-mama's Famous B-52s xiii

Keggie's Amazing Chocolate Caramel Cookies xiv

K-mama's Haystack Cookies 8

Nana Faubion's Everything Cookies.....................18

Grandmama Debbie's Birthday Cookie Cake 28

Honey's Christmas Cookies................................ 37

Nina Karen's Snickerdoodles..............................46

Grandmother Durham's Soft Sugar Cookies..........56

Mimi Carmen's Icebox Cookies...........................66

Nanny Crawford's Pecan Cookies........................76

Gma Barbie's Anise Drops....................................86

Gigi's Cake-Mix Cookies...................................96

Mamie's Grandmother Chocolate Chip Cookies 105

Great Nanny's Peanut Butter Cookies.................114

Mamaw Lou's Easy Chess Bar 123

Nana Judy's Tea Cakes....................................133

Grandma Carol's Pecan Dainties 141

Mim's Crunchy Oatmeal Cookies 153

Nana Sandy's Beach Cookies.............................163

Mamaw Jo's "Grandma Cookies".......................174

About the Authors

Chrys Howard is a *New York Times* bestselling author with more than one million books in print. She has cowritten two cookbooks and two children's books with *Duck Dynasty*'s Kay Robertson as well as *Strong and Kind* and *Duck Commander Devotions for Kids* with her daughter Korie Robertson. Chrys served as a senior editor and creative director for their family-owned business, Howard Publishing, and has spent over forty-five years working with Christian youth camps, serving as a director for more than thirty years. She enjoys speaking and teaching children, teens, and adults as well as traveling overseas for mission efforts. Chrys hosted a weekly radio show and website titled *It's a Mom Thing* for over ten years and currently cohosts a lifestyle site and podcast titled *Rocking It Grand* with coauthor Shellie Tomlinson. Chrys and her husband, John, live in West Monroe, Louisiana. They have three children, fourteen grandchildren, and five great-grandkids.

Shellie Rushing Tomlinson is a multipublished author, speaker, and farmer's wife known for saying "Life can be hard when it's good, but it's always better when you're laughing." Shellie loves using humor and storytelling as she unpacks biblical truth aimed at helping others discover the lives Jesus died to give them. Jeff Foxworthy endorsed her award-winning humor books *Suck Your Stomach In and Put Some Color On!* and *Sue Ellen's Girl Ain't Fat, She Just Weighs Heavy,* and called her laugh-out-loud funny! Shellie's Christian nonfiction work has been featured on the YouVersion Bible app and Right Now Media, the world's largest library of Bible study video resources, and includes the titles *Heart Wide Open, Devotions for the Hungry Heart,* and *Finding Deep and Wide.* After more than a decade in radio, Shellie now hosts *The Story Table* podcast from her home on the banks of Lake Providence, Louisiana, and shares hosting duties on the popular *Rocking It Grand* podcast with coauthor Chrys Howard. Shellie and her husband, Phil, have two children and six grandchildren.